P   ......on Era
**Hebrew Psalms in Modern Metrical English for
Individuals, Choirs and Congregations
by Adam Carlill**

**Complete Psalter
Anglican Edition**

ISBN: 9781983076534
Imprint: Independently published

"If the Psalms really are –as we often say – the primary hymnbook of the Church, as they were the primary hymnbook of Jesus, it seems pretty important that we have ways of singing them that involve congregations singing them in ways they can feel at home with. Adam's fresh and lively versions provide just that opportunity, and I hope many churches will want to take advantage of them and spread the word about their availability."

Rowan Williams

Hymn Society Bulletin – "Brilliant"

About the Author

Adam Carlill was born in Clacton-on-Sea and was baptized in the local Methodist Church, where he went to Sunday School. He was taken to Evensong at the local Anglican Church from an early age, and joined the church choir when he was 8 years old, forsaking Sunday School in order to sing Matins from the Book of Common Prayer.

After leaving school he took his BA in Theology at Keble College, Oxford, before spending a year as the Dean's volunteer in St. George's Cathedral, Jerusalem. He trained for Anglican ministry at Lincoln Theological College and has been in full-time parish ministry continuously since 1990. He has been the Vicar of St. George's Tilehurst since 1998, becoming additionally the Vicar of the neighbouring parish of St Mary Magdalen's.

In 2013 he received his DPhil in Old Testament Theology at St. Peter's College, Oxford with his thesis Cherubim and Seraphim in the Old Testament, subsequently becoming a member of the Society for Old Testament Study.

Frustrated at not being able to use the psalms in worship more widely, in 2015 Adam decided to do something about it, systematically working through the Hebrew Psalter, translating each psalm into modern metrical English. He is now using these psalms regularly in St George's and St Mary Magdalen's.

Acknowledgements

A project like this is not just the work of one person. Although psalms have been part of my life for many years, there are numerous people to whom I owe a great debt of thanks for their assistance.

Firstly, to Keith Beech-Gruneberg, a fellow member of the Society for Old Testament Study, who meticulously checked my initial translation and first metrical draft to make sure it reflected the Hebrew poem as closely as possible. Secondly, to the many musicians who assisted with the prosody, choice of tunes, and other practical aspects of making these poems singable: Judith Ward, Michael Howell, Ian Westley and Richard Mayers. I am indebted to them for their detailed comments, which have improved the quality of this translation immensely. Any faults that remain, however, are my own.

Others who were willing to read or sing the psalms, and gave feedback, were Alex Byrne, Adam Holden, Kate Holden, Bruce von Kugelgen and Alicia von Kugelgen. Members of the Hymn Society of Great Britain and Northern Ireland were unfailingly supportive in their critique of the project, and I am grateful for their good humour and enthusiasm for the psalms.

The congregations of Tilehurst St. George and St. Mary Magdalen have been brilliant. When yet another set of psalms appeared for them to sing they welcomed them and were lovingly fair in their feedback. Without them these psalms would not have seen the light of day. In particular my thanks go to Paul Rowlands and Mary Munday, their respective organists, who always maintained a positive attitude to the project.

Finally, and chief among others that I could mention, are: the members of my cell group, Susan Shooter, Ruth Oates, and Paul Hunt, all of whose love and encouragement have been hugely energising; my Dad, Richard Carlill, who generously pulled in old favours to help out, my Mum, Val, from whom I probably received my artistic bent; and, above all to Gill, Harriet and Ranulph, as always, for being there and not being too put out by Dad spending yet another hour singing and re-singing psalms.

Adam Carlill, March 2018

Psalms for the Common Era: Introduction

The intention of this translation of the psalms is to encourage more people to sing more psalms more often. While the traditions of Anglican chant, responsorial chant and plainsong chant provide us with a rich musical heritage, for many people these forms are inaccessible. One can never please everybody, but by choosing hymn tunes from widely used hymn books, I hope to increase the likelihood that some people will sing the translations of psalms in this book who otherwise would miss out. Most psalms were meant to be sung and there are several tunes mentioned in the ancient Hebrew titles. These suggest that the tunes existed independently of the psalms, as they do here. I have suggested usually one tune for each psalm and made the translation with that tune in mind. I have chosen several tunes for the twenty-two parts of the long alphabetic Psalm 119 for the sake of variety. The choice of tune for the psalms took into consideration primarily the structure and metre of the Hebrew psalm (more of which below), but also the mood and theme.

This psalter is unabridged. As such it is intended as a metrical equivalent of the *Parish Psalter* (Nicholson; The Faith Press: Leighton Buzzard, 1932) and its successors. Inevitably, when translating Hebrew metre into English rhyme, the phrases and ideas frequently do not fit. Where necessary I have embellished the psalm to solve this issue rather than omitting sections. It was a high priority to make sure that the entire psalm was included each time. One of the reasons why metrical psalms are not used as much as they might be is because they frequently skim over difficult or unedifying passages, and, as a result, are often seen as inferior to literal translations. I have not made it my business to decide which psalms, or portions of psalms, are palatable, but to leave such choices to the reader, singer, worship group or congregation. In worship some verses will need to be omitted.

I have tried to follow the voice of each psalm, switching from first to second or third person as the source text demands. The translation is gender neutral with some exceptions: the divine epithets, 'Lord', 'King' and 'Father of the Years' (more on this below) are clearly male, and I have allowed male references to God to stand. To remove all references to 'his', 'he' and 'him' in these instances would be so convoluted as to be unworkable, and would also result in a translation which ended up bearing little relation to the Hebrew poem. Some of the psalms refer to the earthly king of Judah/Israel, and I felt I would be changing an essential part of the text if I were to remove these. Psalm 78 contains two interesting exceptions. In the 11th stanza the Hebrew of verse 31, to which it refers, implies that the objects of God's wrath were first and foremost the male leadership. I have taken advantage of this to use the phrase 'men of note'. Similarly my use of the 'sons of God' (9th stanza for verse 25) interprets 'the mighty ones' as the heavenly court (cf. Job 1-2, 1 Kings 22, etc.) who are referred to as gender specific in Genesis 6.1-2. Occasionally there is gender specific language in direct speech (usually of imagined enemies speaking about the psalmist). On these occasions I have kept 'him' and 'his', etc. but placed these words in italics to indicate that it would be entirely appropriate to replace the word with a feminine pronoun, should that be appropriate to the person using the psalm.

I have paid particular attention to divine names and epithets. The use of Yahweh or Elohim is nearly always reflected in the translation. It is particularly noticeable where psalms have been duplicated and the divine names changed: Psalms 14 (// 53) and 40.14-end (// 70). The divine name, El, is frequently rendered with the Ugaritic title 'Father of the Years' or something that reflects this ancient name.

I have followed the Hebrew numbering, and, as is usual with liturgical psalters, have omitted the ancient headings that are found in the Bible. I have also ignored the untranslatable word 'Selah' which occurs frequently in Hebrew poetry. Alphabetic psalms have been rendered alphabetically: Pss. 9-10, 25, 34, 37, 111, 112, 119 and 145. Because the Hebrew alphabet only contains 22 letters, I have omitted Q, X, Y and Z. This gives the English-speaking reader the opportunity to experience the poem with this rather dispassionate structure in mind.

While I have tried to be true to the Hebrew text, on occasion I have followed the other ancient witnesses to solve some difficultly or corruption. One new addition to the text is the occasional inclusion of an updated cosmology. Fossils, Einsteinian physics and the second law of thermodynamics are all present. This may sound like an odd idea, but this translation is a rendering for the Twenty-first Century, and I wanted the reader to feel that scientific truth is no less a part of God's truth. Modern concepts do not replace biblical ones, but exist alongside them. Biblical writers describe contradictory ideas about the world around them, because, unlike the modern mind, they apparently did not feel it necessary to harmonise myth and reality. The two coexisted, and that is reflected in the use of mythical imagery alongside scientific language here.

A word about Hebrew metre and the process of translation. I began each translation with a literal rendering into English from the Massoretic Text, noting the number of stress units in each verse. This is not an exact science, but it does give some idea of the balance and flow of the poem. Next, I grouped the verses into appropriate sections, depending on the content, and checked to see whether the sections were roughly equal size in terms of the number of stress units. If they were, a suitable English metre was assigned to the psalm before choosing a particular tune to fit. If the psalm were more complicated, I used other devices to find a solution. Sometimes I would take one verse and use it as a refrain (eg. Psalms 5, 7, 8, 45, 48, 120 and 144). Sometimes I would embellish the psalm in places to fit the English metre. A notable example of this is my treatment of Psalm 29, in which one word, 'glory', is expanded into an entire eight-line stanza. These embellishments reflect the content of the Psalm, or make reference to other content in the Hebrew Bible, which I consider appropriate to the psalm. For instance, I have added alleluias to Psalm 100. Although these are not to be found in the psalm, they fit the tone and, in the case of the tune *Victory*, the single syncopated alleluia at the end of each stanza feels very much like the *teru'a*, the victory shout, which is called for at the beginning of the opening verse.

I have taken advantage of the fact that the proper nouns, Sinai and Israel, can be pronounced with either two or three syllables: 'Seye-neye' / 'Seye-nee-eye'; 'Is-rail' / 'Is-ray-el'. I have not indicated in the text which way they should be pronounced, but rely on the rhythm of the line to make this clear to the singer. Similarly I have avoided the use of a grave over the second 'e' of blessed, and trust that the rhythm makes clear which pronunciation should be used. To aid the singer I have tried to use one or the other of these options consistently within each individual psalm.

Translation is the art of compromise. While the principles of the translation are set out here, inevitably there are occasions when the rules I have set myself have been bent a little. However, I hope these psalms prove to be edifying and enable more people to enjoy singing psalms individually or in public, but, either way, making music to God in their hearts, and enjoying the many blessings that he gives.

Adam Carlill, March 2018

Introduction to Canticles for Use at Morning and Evening Prayer

The metrical versions of canticles offered here are of the canticles used in the Book of Common Prayer. Although many member churches of the Anglican Communion have greatly increased the number of biblical and non-biblical canticles in their prayer books, in line with ancient Christian tradition, I have refrained from working on the wider body of material at this stage, in order to keep this volume easy to use. It is intended that this volume may be used to replace all the psalms and canticles that are included in the Book of Common Prayer, so that people may easily sing a simple office without the need for specialist musical training.

Adam Carlill, June 2018

Contents

Canticles for Use at Morning and Evening Prayer

Venite (Psalm 95)

10 11 11 12
Slane

Come, let us ring out our joy to the Lord,
with cheering, thanksgiving and shouting to God,
our rock and salvation to whom we resort,
our King and great Father of the heavenly court.

God's is the power that fashioned the earth,
and brought all the peaks of the mountains to birth,
who made the wide oceans and all they contain,
establishing dry land and the natural domain.

Come, let us honour, bow down and revere
the Lord, who has made us, and kneel down in fear,
for we are his sheep in the pasture of God,
protected and guided by a merciful rod.

[O that today you would listen to me!
Do not close your heart as they did by the sea.
Your forebears at Massah, and Meribah's well,
ignoring my wonders, fell away and rebelled.

Forty years long I despised them and said,
'This people are erring in heart and in head,
not knowing my ways,' so in anger I stressed,
'These rebels will never ever enter my rest.']

Easter Anthems and Gloria

66 66 88
Little Cornard

Christ is the Lamb of God,
slain for the holy feast.
Slaves of the iron rod,
out with the evil yeast!
For we will rise with Christ to reign,
if honesty and truth remain.

Raising the dead on high,
filling with life and breath,
Jesus will never die,
Lord over sin and death.
Regard yourselves as sacrificed,
alive to God in Jesus Christ.

Christ is alive indeed,
yield of the sleeping dead.
Death is of mortal seed,
so too the living bread.
For as in Adam none survive,
in Christ shall all be made alive.

Glory to God above,
Father of all the earth;
praise to the God of love,
Jesus, of human birth;
to God the Spirit glory be,
our risen life eternally.

Te Deum Laudamus
13 13 13 13 13 13
Thaxted

We praise you, God of heaven, acknowledge you as Lord,
the Father everlasting, by all the earth adored.
Continually the angels, with Cherubim and thrones,
with Seraphim and powers, the heavens all intone,
Most holy, holy, holy is God, the Lord of hosts;
your glory fills creation and heavens' furthest coasts.

Your holy church acclaims you in every time and place -
we praise you with apostles, who see your glorious face;
we praise you with the prophets, blessed company of truth;
we praise you with the martyrs, who nobly gave their
youth:
in majesty, the Father; his glorious, only Son;
the Advocate, the Spirit; eternal three in one.

You are the King of Glory, the Father's Son and Christ;
in love you chose to free us when you were sacrificed,
accepting from the Virgin her womb and human birth,
you opened wide your kingdom by bitter death on earth;
enthroned beside the Father, in glory you remain,
to judge the faith of nations when you return again.

Deliver us, the people for whom you paid the price;
enrol us with the saints in eternal paradise.
Lord, bless your holy portion, exalt us as we pray;
direct us as we worship, revere you day by day.
Have mercy, Lord, be gracious, preserve us free from sin;
we trust in you; protect us from shame and guilt within.

Benedicite and Gloria (Short Version)
10 10 10 10
Anima Christi, Ellers, Song 22, Farley Castle,

All of creation, magnify the Lord,
bless him forever, praise with one accord.
Angelic forces, magnify the Lord,
bless him forever, praise with one accord.

You shining heavens, magnify the Lord,
you endless waters, magnify the Lord,
you thrones and powers, magnify the Lord,
bless him forever, praise with one accord.

You sun and moon, come, magnify the Lord,
you stars of heaven, magnify the Lord,
you rain and showers, magnify the Lord,
bless him forever, praise with one accord.

You mighty tempests, magnify the Lord,
You fire and heatwave, magnify the Lord,
winter and summer, magnify the Lord,
bless him forever, praise with one accord.

Moisture and hoarfrost, magnify the Lord,
you freezing cold, come, magnify the Lord,
you snow and ice, come, magnify the Lord,
bless him forever, praise with one accord.

Nighttime and daytime, magnify the Lord,
you light and darkness, magnify the Lord,
you cloud and lightning, magnify the Lord.
bless him forever, praise with one accord.

Let all the earthbound magnify the Lord.
You hills and mountains, magnify the Lord,
all vegetation, magnify the Lord,
bless him forever, praise with one accord.

You wells and fountains, magnify the Lord,
you seas and oceans, magnify the Lord,
you whales and fishes, magnify the Lord,
bless him forever, praise with one accord.

Birds in the heavens, magnify the Lord,
wild beasts and cattle, magnify the Lord,
all men and women, magnify the Lord.
bless him forever, praise with one accord.

Let all of Israel magnify the Lord.
Priests of the Lord, come, magnify the Lord,
all you, his servants, magnify the Lord,
bless him forever, praise with one accord.

You who are righteous, magnify the Lord,
holy and humble, magnify the Lord,
you three companions, magnify the Lord,
bless him forever, praise with one accord.

Come, bless the Father, magnify the Lord.
Come, bless the Son and magnify the Lord.
Come, bless the Spirit, magnify the Lord,
bless him forever, praise with one accord.

Benedicite and Gloria (Long Version)
10 10 10 10
Anima Christi, Ellers, Song 22, Farley Castle,

All of creation, magnify the Lord,
bless him forever, praise with one accord.
Angelic forces, magnify the Lord,
bless him forever, praise with one accord.

You shining heavens, magnify the Lord,
bless him forever, praise with one accord.
You endless waters, magnify the Lord,
bless him forever, praise with one accord.

You thrones and powers, magnify the Lord,
bless him forever, praise with one accord.
You sun and moon, come, magnify the Lord,
bless him forever, praise with one accord.

You stars of heaven, magnify the Lord,
bless him forever, praise with one accord.
You rain and showers, magnify the Lord,
bless him forever, praise with one accord.

You mighty tempests, magnify the Lord,
bless him forever, praise with one accord.
You fire and heatwave, magnify the Lord,
bless him forever, praise with one accord.

Winter and summer, magnify the Lord,
bless him forever, praise with one accord.
Moisture and hoarfrost, magnify the Lord,
bless him forever, praise with one accord.

You freezing cold, come, magnify the Lord,
bless him forever, praise with one accord.
You snow and ice, come, magnify the Lord,
bless him forever, praise with one accord.

Nighttime and daytime, magnify the Lord,
bless him forever, praise with one accord.
You light and darkness, magnify the Lord,
bless him forever, praise with one accord.

You cloud and lightning, magnify the Lord,
bless him forever, praise with one accord.
Let all the earthbound magnify the Lord,
bless him forever, praise with one accord.

You hills and mountains, magnify the Lord,
bless him forever, praise with one accord.
All vegetation, magnify the Lord,
bless him forever, praise with one accord.

You wells and fountains, magnify the Lord,
bless him forever, praise with one accord.
You seas and oceans, magnify the Lord,
bless him forever, praise with one accord.

You whales and fishes, magnify the Lord,
bless him forever, praise with one accord.
Birds in the heavens, magnify the Lord,
bless him forever, praise with one accord.

Wild beasts and cattle, magnify the Lord,
bless him forever, praise with one accord.
All men and women, magnify the Lord,
bless him forever, praise with one accord.

Let all of Israel magnify the Lord,
bless him forever, praise with one accord.
Priests of the Lord, come, magnify the Lord,
bless him forever, praise with one accord.

All you, his servants, magnify the Lord,
bless him forever, praise with one accord.
You who are righteous, magnify the Lord,
bless him forever, praise with one accord.

You who are humble, magnify the Lord,
you who are holy, magnify the Lord,
you three companions, magnify the Lord,
bless him forever, praise with one accord.

Come, bless the Father, magnify the Lord.
Come, bless the Son and magnify the Lord.
Come, bless the Spirit, magnify the Lord,
bless him forever, praise with one accord.

Benedictus and Gloria
87 87 337
Michael

Bless the Lord and God of Israel,
here to set his people free,
raising up a mighty Saviour,
holding royal David's key.
Prophets told
this of old,
end of hatred, evil's hold.

He recalls his holy covenant,
mercy promised long ago,
sworn to Abraham, our father,
freeing from the hateful foe.
We revere,
safe from fear,
just and holy year by year.

You, my child, will go before him,
prophet of the Lord Most High,
making known his saving mercy,
covering sin and evil eye,
dawning light,
peace in sight,
end of death and darkest night.

Glory be to God the Father,
glory be to God the Son,
glory to the Holy Spirit,
ever Three and ever One.
Shore to shore
we adore,
praising you for evermore.

Magnificat and Gloria
87 87 D
Golden Sheaves

My spirit magnifies the Lord,
rejoices in my Saviour.
All generations will record,
that he has shown me favour.
I will be blessed from pole to pole,
though I am poor and lowly,
for he has magnified my soul,
whose mighty name is holy.

His mercy rests on those who fear,
in every generation.
The proud disperse when he is near,
in vain imagination.
He fills the hungry, but disowns
the empty rich, who stumble;
he tears the mighty from their thrones,
exalts the meek and humble.

Remembering Israel by his plan,
his merciful endeavour,
the promise made to Abraham,
and to his seed forever,
he is eternally confessed,
enrolled in sacred pages.
To Father, Son, and Spirit blessed,
be glory down the ages.

Nunc Dimittis and Gloria

86 88 66
Repton, Logan (suegilmurray@icloud.com)

Lord, now you let me die in peace,
fulfilling your decree,
for my own eyes behold today
salvation ready to display,
for everyone to see,
for everyone to see.

Your glory shines in all the world,
with splendour none can quell.
You are their universal light,
among the nations in our sight,
the praise of Israel,
the praise of Israel.

Lord, you will let me die in peace,
for I have seen your face.
To God the Father, God the Son,
and God the Spirit, ever one,
be praise through time and space,
be praise through time and space.

The Psalter

Psalm 1
CM
Richmond

Blessed are the ones who do not walk
in plans of wicked folk,
who do not stand for sinful talk,
or sit with those who mock.

Joyfully they will muse before
their Lord, with great delight;
they meditate upon his law,
unceasing day and night.

Standing like avenues of trees,
where streams and rivers flow,
they never wither, and with ease,
they flourish there and grow.

Not so, the wicked folk, not so!
Their evil schemes decay.
As dust or chaff, the wind will blow
and drive them all away.

Knowing them all, the Lord will raise
the righteous and their sort.
May sinners die, and all their ways,
before the righteous court.

Psalm 2

87 87 D
Ebenezer (Ton-Y-Botel)

Why the global agitation,
empty speeches, all in vain?
Kings and worldly leaders gather;
what can they intend to gain?
Close together, they conspire to
bring the Lord's anointed down.
'We will break their cords that bind us!' -
sacred cords and holy crown.

God in heaven reigns securely,
sits enthroned above in might,
snorts derision in their faces,
scorns their plotting, hateful spite.
Wrath and anger leave them pale and
petrified, as still as stone.
'Sanctity resides in Zion,
heaven's monarch on the throne.'

God, the Lord, has made a statute;
I will tell you what he said:
'You, my only child and heir, will
rule the nations in my stead.
Ask me, and you will receive the
peoples of the earth, to own.
Break them with an iron rod, and
shatter them, in pieces sown.'

So be careful, all you rulers;
be admonished, you who lead.
Wait for God with apprehension,
as with prudence you proceed.
Burning anger will consume the
evil and imperfect path.
Blessed are those who seek his refuge,
who avoid his fearful wrath.

Psalm 3
LM
Breslau

Lord, how innumerable my foes,
who wish to take away my life!
So many rise, who presuppose
you cannot rescue me from strife.

Yet you, my God, lift up my face,
and shield me with your glorious light.
I plead within your holy place,
and you give answer in my sight.

But as for me, repose is mine;
I sleep and wake, as God restores.
I do not fear, though bands combine,
and thousands gather at my door.

Rise, Lord, to save, my God, to bless.
You smite my foes, their evil jaws.
You break the teeth of wickedness.
Release and blessing - they are yours!

Psalm 4
10 4 10 4 10 10
Sandon, Alberta

O God I call! Give heed and let me hear
your gracious word.
In narrow paths you ease my way to prayer,
my righteous Lord.
How long, you torpid souls, will you remain
in love with lies, pursuing them in vain?

Know how my Lord will pour on faithful souls
his marvellous deeds.
He hears and answers, when they rise and call;
he meets their needs.
Let not your trembling soul incline to ill,
consider him, and on your bed be still.

Offer the Lord your blameless gift in peace,
and rest assured.
Though many fear, and entropy increase,
their minds inured,
I trust in you, my Lord, and seek your face.
Lift up your light, and send your saving grace.

You give me pleasure, as you set me free
within my soul.
Sweeter than sustenance, or growth, to me
is your control.
In even peace and stillness I may rest,
in you, my Lord, to lie secure and blessed.

Psalm 5
CM
Binchester

Listen, O Lord! Answer my cry;
discern my earnest care.
Consider me, my King and God,
as now I make my prayer.

When I awake, calling to you;
I watch and make my claim.
For you despise unrighteousness,
dispelling evil aims.

Those who are proud cannot remain
before your searching gaze,
for you abhor their hands of blood,
and their deceitful ways.

Only by grace can I give praise,
approach your house with awe.
Your favour, Lord, will be a crown,
my shield for evermore.

Lord, make my ways truthful and straight,
because of cunning spies,
whose faithless tongues and secret lusts
are graves and empty lies.

Sentence them, Lord; drive out their plans,
their horde of wilful sin.
May those, who love and seek your shade,
rejoice and ever sing.

Only by grace can I give praise,
approach your house with awe.
Your favour, Lord, will be a crown,
my shield for evermore.

Psalm 6
77 77 D
Aberystwyth

Lord, my God, do not contend;
do not castigate and chide.
May your grace and life extend
soothing touch and balm inside.
Terrified and never free,
how long must I wait in vain?
Turn around to rescue me.
Save me! Let your love remain.

Who in death remembers you;
shades can never offer praise.
Weariness is all I know,
sleepless nights and tearful days.
See my endless waking sighs;
how long must I wait in vain,
while vexation wastes my eyes,
weakened in my constant pain?

Turn away from me, my foes,
you who work with evil spite.
God has heard my grievous throes,
endless crying, day and night.
May my enemies beware,
shamed and fearful, never free.
God will hear my humble prayer;
he will act upon my plea.

Psalm 7
666 66 and Refrain
Personent Hodie (Theodoric)

Lord, my God, rescue me;
you alone hear my plea,
lest my foes capture me,
pierce my soul with iron,
tearing like a lion.

I will praise, praise, praise;
I will sing, sing, sing:
God is high, God is true;
praise the God of justice!

If my hands deal in wrong,
if my deeds all along
spoil my friends, hurt the strong,
may my life be taken,
lie in dust, forsaken.

I will praise, praise, praise;
I will sing, sing, sing:
God is high, God is true;
praise the God of justice!

Rise, O God, take your stand;
foes are near, close at hand;
be our judge, give command;
summon all the peoples
to your throne as equals.

I will praise, praise, praise;
I will sing, sing, sing:
God is high, God is true;
praise the God of justice!

Judge me, Lord; your decree
will uphold honesty.
You destroy cruelty,
certify the faithful;
you appraise the graceful.

I will praise, praise, praise;
I will sing, sing, sing:
God is high, God is true;
praise the God of justice!

God redeems upright hearts;
he will shield inward parts,
making sharp sword and darts,
ire for empty penance,
fire and deadly sentence.

I will praise, praise, praise;
I will sing, sing, sing:
God is high, God is true;
praise the God of justice!

As for those who despise,
hatching ill, spawning lies;
these become their demise;
none then ever spare them;
violence will ensnare them.

I will praise, praise, praise;
I will sing, sing, sing:
God is high, God is true;
praise the God of justice!

Psalm 8
10 4 66 66 10 4
Luckington

How great your name, in all the earth adored,
exalted Lord!
From babe to heaven's throne,
your majesty they own,
to quell the vengeful heart,
and foes who stand apart.
How great your name, in all the earth adored,
exalted Lord!

How great your name, in all the earth adored,
exalted Lord!
From age and endless years,
your contrapuntal spheres,
you stoop to hear our groan,
in dust and ashes sown.
How great your name, in all the earth adored,
exalted Lord!

How great your name, in all the earth adored,
exalted Lord!
No deity can name
our noble human frame.
We supervise and know
your natural earth below.
How great your name, in all the earth adored,
exalted Lord!

How great your name, in all the earth adored,
exalted Lord!
You give into our care
your creatures, rich and rare;
your mysteries are profound,
unfathomable ground.
How great your name, in all the earth adored,
exalted Lord!

Psalm 9 (An Alphabetic Psalm, Part 1)
LM
Conditor Alme Siderum, Veni Creator Spiritus (Mechlin)

All thanks to you, my Lord of grace,
with all my heart in time and space.
Again, let me rejoice and sing
your mighty name, O highest King.

Before your face my foes retreat,
and fall prostrate beneath your feet.
Before your throne a fair reply
upholds the justice of my cry.

Consuming nations' wickedness,
rebuking them when they oppress,
committing them to loss and shame,
you wipe out every hateful name.

Detractors fall, exhausted, down,
like empty ruins, ploughed and sown.
Domains, uprooted by your hand,
are out of thought, in dust and sand.

Enacting judgements that endure,
the Lord will ever reign secure,
enveloping the world with truth
and equity, for age and youth.

For those who bear abuse and pain,
the Lord is castle and domain.
For those who know and trust you still,
you hold them close, their prayers fulfil.

Go out and sing the Lord's decrees,
and tell the peoples of his deeds.
Go now! He keeps the poor in mind,
protecting needy humankind.

Hear and restore me, Lord of life!
When foes attack, survey my strife.
Here I recount your victory praise,
in Zion's gates your saving ways.

Immersed within their pits and snares,
their hordes lie taken unawares.
In righteous deeds the Lord is known;
by him the vile are overthrown.

Just as the wicked turn from God,
in Sheol they are overawed.
Judge, Lord, arise and take your stand,
to bring the peoples back in hand.

Kept by the poor, their hope is blessed,
by God eternally confessed.
Keep faith, and make the nations know
that they are human here below.

Psalm 10 (An Alphabetic Psalm, Part 2)
LM
Conditor Alme Siderum, Veni Creator Spiritus (Mechlin)

Look down, O Lord, do not ignore!
Why hide your presence from the poor?
Laboriously the wicked plan;
bring down the counsels they began.

Majestic precepts they ignore;
while snorting pride, they stand secure.
Myopic folk, in heart they say,
'No curse can undermine our way.'

No curse, but boasting theft and pride,
'There is no God,' they say inside,
'nor can he see or call to mind;
he hides away from humankind.'

Perfidiously they hide away,
and, crouching down to catch their prey,
pick off with nets the helpless poor,
by captains crouching at their door.

Repulsive plots preoccupy
their mouths and minds and evil eye.
Reclusive in the rural town,
they lurk to drag the sinless down.

Transcendent Lord, lift up your hand;
remember justice, take your stand.
The wicked spurn you every day,
they think that you will not repay.

Upon the earth you see the pain,
regard the anger and the strain.
Unless the orphans look to you,
no other help will see them through.

Vindictive armies, Lord, erase,
and hide away their wicked ways.
Vouchsafe to rule for evermore;
restrain the foe to reign secure.

Whenever aching prayers ascend
from anxious hearts, you comprehend.
When, crushed in terror, orphans cry,
you give them justice from on high.

Psalm 11
66 86 SM
Narenza, Franconia

To God I look for help,
a stronghold at my side.
So, how then can you say to me,
'Fly to the hills, and hide.

'For look, the wicked stand,
with ready bow and dart,
to shoot from sin and shadow at
the upright pure in heart.

'When strong foundations fall,
and powers that be lie prone,
what can the righteous do or say?
The blameless are undone!'?

The Lord within his shrine
is sitting high above,
to look on earth and cast around,
examine and reprove.

The Lord considers yet
humanity's intent.
Abhoring all their violence, he
demands that they repent.

And when the judgement falls,
with snares and scorching rain,
the wicked are rebuked, and wrath
shall be their cup to drain.

The Lord is ever just,
approving righteous ways.
The upright see, and they confess
his vision in their days.

Psalm 12
665 665 786
Jesu, Meine Freude

Godliness is failing,
faithfulness is ailing;
save me, God of truth!
Emptiness they utter,
oily lips that mutter
doublespeak, and smooth.
End their slippery lips and tongues,
their bravado and pretension,
boasting and invention!

'Tongues may be prevailing,
lips may be assailing,
overbearing lords.
When the poor are groaning,
when the weak are moaning,
I will hear their words.
I will rise up to release
those, who yearn for liberation,
be their vindication.'

Silver, purest brightness,
incandescent whiteness,
are the words of God.
You, Lord, will direct them,
cover and protect them,
from the evil horde,
even though the wicked stalk
all around, with base ambition,
empty of contrition.

Psalm 13
10 10 10 10
Heswall

How long, O Lord my God, will you forget?
How long, must I endure till you abet?
How long shall schemes and grief invade the mind?
How long shall foes arise to undermine?

Look down, my Lord, on me, my every breath.
Look down and give me light; I sleep in death;
lest my opponents overwhelm below,
rejoice among themselves, and bring me low.

But I, I trust in you, your clemency;
may I rejoice in you - you set me free.
Forever I will sing to you, my Lord,
for you have ever been my full reward.

Psalm 14
887
Stabat Mater

Fools deny their God within them,
while they work licentious mayhem;
there is no-one virtuous.

Then the Lord from heaven descended,
and our nature comprehended:
was there thought or thirst for God?

All have turned away together,
fraudulent in their endeavour,
no-one upright here at all.

Wicked people have no knowledge,
as they swallow those in bondage.
They do not proclaim the Lord.

All the wicked shall be daunted,
and by fear and terror haunted;
God is with his faithful heirs.

Though you ridicule our vision,
spoil the poor in their submission,
he, the Lord, is their defence.

Who will give relief from Zion,
freeing captives from their prison?
May his people all rejoice!

Psalm 15
87 87 87 8
Corde Natus (Divinum Mysterium)

Lord, who may approach your temple,
dwell upon your holy hill?
Those who walk in blameless pathways,
those whose deeds are righteous still;
those who speak the truth sincerely,
those whose tongues are free from ill:
folk like this shall not be shaken.

Those who never hurt a neighbour,
nor reproach their friends near by;
those who see themselves as lowly,
while they raise the faithful high;
those who tell the truth at all times,
free from fraud and greedy eye:
folk like this shall not be shaken.

Psalm 16
CM
Westminster

O Lord and Father, keep me safe,
for you are my retreat.
Without you, all my passing wealth
is nothing, incomplete.

But as for holy ones in power,
and great beyond belief,
they squander all your land affords,
and multiply their grief.

They pour libations to their gods,
but I will not partake,
for guiltless blood is daily poured
around them, in their wake.

The Lord alone is all I have,
my heritage bestowed.
My share of land is wonderful,
a beautiful abode.

I bless the Lord who counsels me,
advising me by night.
With this in mind I dwell secure,
forever in your sight.

So now my heart and soul rejoice,
my flesh shall rest secure;
you keep me from the pit, to live
with those whose lives are pure.

For you reveal the path of life,
felicity in store,
eternity before your face,
and joy for evermore.

Psalm 17
10 10 10 10 10 10
Finlandia

My Lord, pay heed to justice; be aware.
Empty and poor, I raise my cry to you.
Stretch forth your ear; I honestly declare;
no treacherous lips or evil to review.
May judgement stand, and justice be revealed.
Before your court I make my last appeal.

You try my heart, and visit in the night.
As I await, you search me to the core.
Although your gaze brings wickedness to light,
I have no lie, no defect to deplore,
no human deals, no action or device,
no conscience seared, or evil sacrifice.

I hear your word, O Father of the Years,
while I have seen the pathways of the vile.
You hold my path, and keep at bay the fears;
my steps are firm, though evil may beguile.
And when I call, you hear me and defend;
yes, when I call, you answer and attend.

My Lord, give ear to me; may love apply;
in mercy listen; you are my retreat.
Keep me in mind, the apple of an eye;
your wings above, you hide me safe beneath.
Though foes destroy, and wickedness abound,
your strong right hand will hold my life around.

Obese in heart, they boast of their renown;
they set their eyes to leer within the land.
Like hungry lions, hidden underground,
they long to maul, their actions underhand.
Rise up, my Lord, rebuke them and abase;
make them bow down, confront them face to face.

Lord, save my soul, when wicked folk abound;
lift up your sword on those, who are the great,
who have their fill, with treasures all around;
their children stand to gain a grand estate.
But I will wake, to see you close beside,
your righteous face will keep me satisfied.

Psalm 18
66 84 D
Leoni

I love you, God my Lord,
my stronghold and my rock,
my refuge, my eternal ward
and sturdy lock,
my ancient keep and wall,
my fortress and retreat;
I praise and call you, Lord of all,
my victory seat.

The cords of death confound,
and fill me with dismay;
the waves of chaos roll around
their trembling prey.
From Sheol's awesome void
they tighten and control,
and deadly snares have near destroyed
my heart and soul.

Yet from my grim distress
to God my prayers emerge,
although the floods of worthlessness
appal and surge;
I call with one accord,
that he may hear my cry,
and from the temple of the Lord
he makes reply.

Foundations of the earth
are shaken to the core;
volcanic strata writhe in birth
at Sheol's door;
they tremble at his rage
and incandescent ire,
which blazes out from age to age,
a searing fire.

He tears apart the skies,
a storm beneath his feet,
and, darting on the wind, he flies
through hail and sleet;
in darkness he descends,
and, charging through the cloud,
his cherubim below extend
their whirling shroud.

His splendour shines around,
and, breaking through the sky,
the thunders of the Lord resound
from God Most High.
In mighty, rushing wind
his tempest roars aloud;
and lightning scatters humankind,
ashamed and cowed.

The deepest ocean shores
lie naked and exposed,
and long-forgotten dinosaurs
become disclosed;
you blast them with your breath,
the waters boil and foam.
He drew me up from certain death,
to bring me home.

The Lord will save my life,
from those who push and press,
with hardened face and endless strife,
in my distress.
From suffocating straits,
to favour and delight,
he brought me through eternal gates
to space and light.

The Lord is my success,
according to my due;
my innocence and righteousness
are all in view.
My thoughts are free from shame;
I live by all his laws.
I have not disavowed his name
for any cause.

His laws are in my mind,
his statutes in my heart;
from evil ways I am confined
in every part.
The Lord is my success,
according to my due;
my innocence and righteousness
are still in view.

The kind in heart obtain
your kindness from above,
and perfect ones forever gain
your perfect love;
for purity you give
a pure and peaceful state,
but, to the twisted, who deceive,
a devious fate.

You save the humble poor,
derisive looks bring low;
you light my lamp, O Lord, and pour
your light below.
Battalions on the march
are totally devoured;
by God the well-protected arch
is overpowered.

The Father of the Years
is perfect, good and kind,
eternal shield, who calms the fears
of humankind;
for there is only one,
our refuge and reward,
to those who seek, a shield and sun,
our God and Lord.

The Father of the Years
has girded me with power.
Perfecting all my ways, he clears
terrain and tower.
Surefooted, as a doe
upon a rocky crest,
I run and stretch a brazen bow,
to meet the test.

My saviour and my ward
against a mad crusade,
surrounding me, your arm and sword
will give me aid;
your lowliness and grace
have made me great in might,
enlarging every step I place
in land and fight.

Harassing all my foes,
and, hounding their retreat,
I give no quarter and impose
their full defeat.
I lay them in the dust,
and, rising up no more,
their names reduce to nothing, just
a prize of war.

You girded me with power,
tenacious in the fight,
and all who rise in malice cower
or turn in flight,
with no-one to surround,
unanswered by the Lord,
outpoured upon the miry ground,
unseen, unheard.

You draw me from dispute
and overwhelming war;
my name is held in great repute;
I dwell secure.
Emerging from their forts,
the nations, they obey;
exhausted in my noble courts,
they melt away.

So, blessed be God my Lord,
my battlement and wall,
who rises up as shield and sword
and God of all.
The Father of the Years,
avenger of the poor,
suppressing hateful foes, appears
for evermore.

You raise me up on high
above my endless foes;
you save me, as the years go by,
from swords and bows.
I celebrate your name,
in every time and place.
You bless your monarch's earthly reign
with heavenly grace.

Psalm 19
85 85 843
Angel Voices

Heaven tells the Father's glory
every passing phase;
stars above declare the story,
all his works and ways;
day by day creation preaches,
and its speech is full of praise.

Silently their voice is sounding
forth, without a word,
and, in all the earth abounding,
languages unheard,
from eternal constellations
to the nations: 'Praise the Lord!'

And the sun, among the voices,
rising from his source,
like a bridegroom, he rejoices
to maintain his course,
blazing onwards in his carriage
to his marriage, vital force.

For the law of God is perfect,
aiding heart and soul,
cheering us in every subject,
altogether whole;
clean and curing, still enduring,
and ensuring self-control.

All your precepts and your judgements
make the simple wise;
all your statutes and commandments
shine upon the eyes,
pure and forthright, sure and upright,
as the daylight in the skies.

More desirable than money,
or the finest gold,
sweeter than the golden honey
any hive can hold,
is the learning they afford, and
their reward cannot be told.

From my secret sins perfect me,
hidden deep inside;
from my vain conceit protect me,
and from haughty pride.
Keep me from the great misdeed, so
I indeed am purified.

May my words and contemplation
rise before your sight.
May my heart and meditation
be your sweet delight.
Only you can still deliver,
rock and giver, Lord of might.

Psalm 20
8 8 9 10
The Truth From Above

The Lord be your defence in strife;
the God of Jacob keep your life,
support your cause, winning every race,
and send you help from Zion's holy place;

remember every gift you bring,
your holy vows, the food of kings;
and give to you all your heart can find,
fulfil your counsels and inform your mind.

May we ring out your victory cry,
and in God's name our banner fly.
The Lord give ear every time you plead,
and answer you in every kind of need.

I know the Lord will now protect
our monarch here, as we expect,
with mighty hand, save and hear your cry,
defend you from his holy heaven on high.

While some trust horses or their arms,
to keep them safe in time of harm,
the Lord our God saves us from the spear;
we make his holy name remembered here.

So now they fall at your command,
but we are risen and will stand.
O Lord, we pray, hear and save the king,
and may he answer daily when we sing.

Psalm 21
LM
Gonfalon Royal

The king rejoices in your might;
because you save him, you are blessed.
You satisfy his appetite,
and, Lord, you answer his request.

You come with blessings to bestow,
you crown his head with purest gold;
from you he sought for life below;
you freely give him days untold.

His glory rising by your aid,
endowed with honour, pride and grace,
by blessing and approval made,
you give him joy before your face.

Our king, you grasp your hostile foes,
uncover those who hate your ways;
and when, in fury bands oppose,
your face will set them all ablaze.

The Lord will swallow down for sure;
his burning wrath devour them all;
their fruit will never grow mature,
until their generations fall.

For they have planned an evil snare,
prepared a scheme to set in place.
Rebuffing them without a care,
you aim your bow before their face.

Our king has trusted you, O Lord,
and by your grace will stand secure.
The Lord is high, in might adored;
we sing and praise you evermore.
Amen.

Psalm 22
87 87 87
Picardy, Mannheim

O my God, my God! Where are you?
Why have you forsaken me?
Why are you so far from saving,
saving me from misery?
God, I need an urgent answer;
I am yearning constantly.

Day by day I call in anguish,
but you do not hear my cry,
peering in the dark for answers,
as my terrors close nearby.
Night and day I seek for silence,
any peace before I die.

You, my God, are pure and holy,
praise of Israel, King on high.
In the past our forebears trusted;
they believed and you stood by.
They were faithful, so you saved them,
turning quickly to reply.

I am just a worm, not human,
scorned and shunned by passers-by.
All who see me stare and mock me,
gawping as they peer and pry.
'Let the Lord protect and save *him*,
save the apple of his eye.'

When my mother was in labour,
you delivered me to birth;
laid me as a helpless baby
at her breast, alive on earth.
I have trusted you, my maker,
since my mother brought me forth.

Do not be so far from helping,
when distress is ever near;
I am all alone and helpless,
in my ever-present fear.
Do not leave me unprotected,
on my own, without you here.

Many bulls are gathering round me,
hemming me on every side,
mighty bulls of Bashan's pastures,
gaping muzzles open wide,
roaring like an angry lion,
tearing at my heart inside.

I am emptied out like water,
poured onto a thirsty field;
while my bones are all disjointed,
pulled apart until I yield.
Heart and soul within are melting;
I believe my fate is sealed.

Now my mouth is dry and dusty,
like a potsherd on the ground,
while my tongue is sore and swollen,
sticking to my gums, and bound.
In the dust of death you place me,
and the shades are drifting round.

Like a pack of dogs they circle,
searching round for food to eat,
evil-doers who surround me,
plotting violence in the street;
with their lion's teeth they maul me,
piercing through my hands and feet.

In my weakness I am starving;
all my bones are standing out,
as they gather round, uncaring;
deaf to me, they come about,
tearing all my clothes among them,
casting lots to share them out.

So, my Lord, do not ignore me;
Lord, be swift to send me aid.
Save my soul from sword and conflict,
growling dog and murderous blade.
From the lions' mouths and oxen,
you have saved me when I prayed.

I declare your name and glory,
praising you among the throng.
You who fear the God of Israel,
praise the Lord in prayer and song.
May the seed of Jacob fear him;
glorify the Lord, be strong.

God has not despised the poorest,
nor detested those in need;
he has not ignored their crying,
or their yearning, as they plead.
All my praise, in open worship,
will proclaim your word and deed.

Now I will fulfil my pledges,
in the presence of the poor;
minister the holy portions,
to the hungry, as I swore.
They will seek the Lord, and praise him,
have their fill for evermore.

All the earth will long remember,
turning to the Lord again;
every country, every nation,
will acknowledge your domain.
You are Lord of all the peoples,
yours the kingdom, yours the reign.

In your kingdom none will hunger,
all will eat your sacred feast;
you will raise their souls to worship,
every one from death released,
heaven and earth and hell together,
from the greatest to the least.

Generations in the future,
serving you in every place,
praising you before their children,
every tribe and every race,
they will tell your righteous wonders,
through the years, in time and space.

Psalm 23
10 10
Song 46

God is my shepherd; nothing shall I need.
In grassy fields he lays me down to feed.

By restful waters he directs my soul,
and gently brings me back to make me whole.

In righteous paths he guides my erring feet,
that I may know his name, for it is sweet.

Yes, though I walk alone in death's dark vale,
I will not fear when evil shall assail.

For you are with me, ever by my side,
your rod and staff to comfort and to guide.

You have arranged a table in my sight,
as witness to my foes of your delight.

Pouring the purest oil upon my head,
you fill my cup, and I am richly fed.

Surely your grace and mercy will pursue;
they daily follow me, my whole life through.

So I will dwell within the holy gate,
for length of days, O Lord, to watch and wait.

Psalm 24
66 86 SM
St. Ethelwald

The Lord controls the earth
and all that it contains;
by his decree the human race
is stable and remains.

Upon eternal floods
he set the mountains fast.
Upon the rivers of the deep
the world is made to last.

Who may approach the Lord,
to see his holy place?
Who may ascend his holy hill,
to stand before his face?

The one whose hands are clean,
the one whose heart is pure,
whose life is not a waste of time,
whose promises are sure.

On those who live like this
come blessings from the Lord,
the God of righteousness, from whom
salvation is assured.

These are the righteous folk,
who seek for Jacob's Lord,
the generation of the just,
who seek your righteous word.

Lift up your heads, O gates;
lift up, eternal doors,
and let the King of Glory in
to your unending shores.

Who is the one who comes,
to enter through these doors?
It is the Lord, the mighty one,
the hero of the wars.

Lift up your heads, O gates;
lift up, eternal doors,
and let the King of Glory in
to your unending shores.

Who is the one who comes,
to enter through these gates?
It is the Lord of angels here;
the King of Glory waits.

Psalm 25 (An Alphabetic Psalm)
65 65
Pastor Pastorum, Eudoxia

All my life, my Maker,
I lift up to you,
for my soul is yours, to
know me through and through.

Be a great assurance;
save me from my shame,
lest my foes deride me,
ridicule my name.

Come to your believers,
save them from their shame;
but the false and faithless,
may they bear the blame.

Deep within my being
make me know your ways;
teach me all your paths, to
follow all my days.

Ever lead me forward,
in your truth and light;
train and teach me, God, and
save me by your might.

Faithfully I waited
all the day for you;
by your loving kindness
keep my life in view.

Give to me compassion,
give your grace, my Lord,
since they stand forever
by your mighty word.

Hide away my guilt, my
sins and childish ways,
for your goodness' sake, my
Lord of endless days.

Innocent and upright
is the Lord above,
therefore sinners learn his
way of life and love.

Justly guiding every
needy, faithful soul,
he will teach the poor his
way of righteous goals.

Kindliness and truth are
pathways of the Lord,
for the folk, who guard his
covenant and his word.

Lord, forgive my error,
endless sin and shame;
then will others praise you,
glorify your name.

Many are the faithful,
whom the Lord has kept,
teaching them the way of
life they should accept.

Near to grace and goodness
they will lodge and stay,
while their seed inherit
regions far away.

Only for the faithful,
who confess the Lord,
are the wisest counsel,
covenant and reward.

Permanently looking,
trusting in the Lord,
he will draw my feet from
nets they spread abroad.

Rise, attend my pleading;
may I know your grace,
for I am alone, and
poor before your face.

Sorrows are increasing,
filling every sigh.
Save me from distresses,
free me from on high.

Take to heart my anguish,
all my tears and toil;
lift me from my sins, that
endlessly embroil.

Understand how many
foes surround my life,
numerous folk who hate me,
savage in their strife.

Visit me to save me;
keep my soul secure;
may I not be shamed, my
refuge and my shore.

While I am awaiting
your redeeming arm,
innocence and honour
keep me free from harm.

Turn towards your people;
ransom Israel;
save us, God, from every
pain and snare of hell.

Psalm 26
10 10 10 10 10 10
Unde et Memores

Give judgement, Lord; consider my appeal.
In my integrity I ever live.
I trust in you, my Lord; to you I kneel,
and so I never slip, but grow and thrive.
Examine me, my Lord; assess my mind,
and may my inmost being be refined.

Your loving-kindness is before my eyes;
my faithfulness to you has never failed.
I never sit with those who worship lies,
or enter in with those whose thoughts are veiled.
I hate the congregations of the vile;
I never sit with those who trust in guile.

I wash my hands in innocency now,
that I may go about your altar, Lord,
to teach a prayer of thanks and honoured vow,
recounting all the wonders of your word.
My Lord, I love the house where you abide,
the glory of your shrine, where you reside.

Protect me when you gather up their souls,
their sinful, bloody hands that bribe and scheme.
Integrity and justice are my goals.
O ransom me, be gracious and redeem.
My foot will stand, in righteousness assured;
among the faithful host I bless the Lord.

Psalm 27
LM
Solothurn, O Lux Beata Trinitas

The Lord is my redeeming light,
the Lord who gives me life and might.
Of whom shall I be trapped in fear?
Whom shall I dread, when they are near?

When evil folk approach in hate,
when wickedness and foes await,
they try to eat my flesh, but they
will fall and stumble far away.

If armies camp and war arise,
surrounding me before my eyes,
my heart within will never fear,
and I will trust that you are near.

The only thing I ask the Lord,
that I will seek as my reward:
to see his beauty all my days,
reside within his house and ways.

When evil comes you hide my life,
within your tent and rock, in strife.
You raise my head above my foes,
who gather round me to enclose.

So I will make a sacrifice,
with joyful shout in paradise,
that I may sing a song of praise
to God, the Lord, for all his ways.

My Lord, attend and hear my sigh;
take notice of my earnest cry;
be gracious to me by your love,
and answer from your throne above.

Of you my heart has spoken clear,
'Go, seek his face in faith and fear.'
And so, I seek your face, my Lord,
your presence and your holy word.

So do not hide your face away,
or bar me in an evil day;
but may your anger turn aside,
for you have been my help and guide.

Do not forsake me, saving God,
and do not leave me overawed.
Though parents spurn - a bitter cup -
the Lord will bow to take me up.

Lord, teach me righteous paths today,
and guide me in your righteous way.
For many stand around, to see
what may befall and injure me.

Do not concede my life to those
who, breathing violent rage, oppose,
for witnesses are speaking lies,
and straining hard for my demise.

The one thing that I still believe,
is, with the living, I receive
a vision of the Lord above,
of goodness and eternal love.

So watch and wait; the Lord is true.
Endure and he will comfort you.
Your heart be strong, your eye be bright,
and wait for everlasting light.

Psalm 28
LM
Veni Creator Spiritus (Mechlin)

To you I cry, my Lord and might;
do not keep silence in my sight,
lest you be still, and I will go
down to the pit, and bending low.

Lord, hear my prayer, my earnest cry;
to you I raise my voice on high;
I lift my hands before your face,
to your abode and holy place.

Do not arrest or drag me down,
with those who trouble me around,
who speak of peace among their friends,
but nurture wicked, evil ends.

Repay them as their deeds deserve,
and as their evil actions serve;
return on them their enterprise,
their unjust deals and compromise.

For they do not discern the Lord,
his art and handiwork and word;
but he will cast them down below,
nor build them up to thrive and grow.

Now let the Lord my God be blessed,
for he regarded my request,
the Lord, my strength and mighty shield,
in whom my confidence is sealed.

For I am helped, my heart delights
to sing his praise, his saving might.
The Lord protects his chosen one,
working salvation from the throne.

Save your own, bless your endeavour,
raise and pasture them for ever.
Amen.

Psalm 29
Irregular
St. Patrick (vv. 1,2,3,5), Gartan (v. 4)

Proclaim the Lord, you heavenly host;
proclaim the Lord of glorious might;
proclaim the Lord, his glorious name;
bow down before his holy light.

The Lord calls out upon the waters,
the call of God in holy splendour;
the Lord upon eternal waters,
the call of God, the great contender;
the call of God in flame of fire,
the God of ever-circling spheres,
with fearsome thunder to inspire,
the ancient Father of the Years.

The call of God destroys the groves,
and smashes trees in Lebanon;
he makes them skip around in droves,
in Lebanon and Sirion.
The call of God, as deserts writhe;
he sets the Kadesh wastes ablaze,
he strips the oak trees like a scythe,
as in his temple all give praise.

['God of glory, God of splendour,
God of might and God of thunder,
God of power, our defender,
God of awe and wonder;
call of God in empty spaces,
call of hope to those forsaken,
call of God in broken places;
call to reawaken.']

Proclaim the Lord, you heavenly host;
proclaim the Lord of glorious might;
proclaim the Lord, his glorious name;
bow down before his holy light.
The Lord is King in age and aeon,
enthroned above the old abyss,
the Lord of might for praise and paean;
the Lord will bless us all with peace.

Psalm 30
LM
Angelus

I raise your praises, Lord, on high,
for you have drawn me from the mire;
foes who surround, with evil eye,
fall back despondent and expire.

O Lord and God, I cried to you;
you healed and saved me from distress,
bringing me up from hell below,
raising my soul from death's abyss.

Make music to the Lord divine,
you faithful folk, who see his face;
offer your praise within the shrine,
for a memorial of his grace.

For anger briefly is in sight,
but favour causes life and heart.
Weeping may lodge into the night;
morning will bring a joyful start.

And as for me, with peace at hand,
I thought that I would never sway;
Lord, by your grace you made me stand,
firm as the hills in every way.

But then you turned away your face,
for I was troubled and afraid.
Then, Lord, I sought your saving grace,
praying for you to give me aid.

What profit is there in my blood,
if I descend to death's abyss?
Can there be praise from clay and mud?
Can we acclaim your truth and bliss?

Lord, hear and turn your gracious glance,
to help when thoughts and fears annoy;
turn all my wailing into dance,
sackcloth and rags to clothes of joy.

So, Lord, your glory is my song;
eternal music will resound.
Lord God, your praise is on my tongue,
with me forever, all around.

Psalm 31
DCM
First Mode Melody

Lord, in your name I seek retreat,
so let me not be shamed.
Answer with justice from your seat,
that I may not be blamed.
Listen to me, be swift to hear;
deliver me from harm,
save me, O God, my rock in fear,
a stronghold in the storm.

You are my castle and my keep,
refresh and comfort me.
Out of their net within the deep,
you reach to set me free.
Into your hands and, free from fears,
I place my age and youth.
Ransom me, Father of the Years,
O Lord and God of truth.

All those who worship lies you hate,
but I will trust in you,
joyful, because the Lord is great,
your loving-kindness true.
You, who have seen my poverty,
you know my soul's distress,
placing me safe from enemy,
away from crush and press.

Lord, show your grace in my distress,
my vexed and fading eye,
churning my soul with deep unrest,
as troubles horrify.
Life is so full of tears and sighs,
lamenting every day;
energy fails and power dies;
my bones consume away.

I am become contemptible
to every hateful foe.
even, like them, unbearable,
to those I used to know.
Kindred and friends all turn away,
avoid me in the street;
fearing to speak in any way,
they beat a swift retreat.

I am forgotten as the dead,
forsaken, out of mind;
shattered and broken in my dread,
and totally resigned,
hearing the whispers, as they speak
of terror all around;
sitting there in an evil clique,
they plan to bring me down.

Lord, I will ever trust in you,
and say, 'You are my God.'
All of my time is in your view,
beneath your hand and rod.
Free me from powerful foes who talk,
who try to capture me.
Shine on me, save me from the hawk;
in mercy set me free.

Lord, let me never be ashamed,
Lord, answer and acquit.
May all the wicked folk be blamed,
and silent in the pit.
May all their lying lips be still,
who speak against the just -
arrogance, pride, contempt - until
they fall and turn to dust.

Great is your goodness, which you store
for praise and piety.
All who seek refuge at your door
before society -
keep them close by, your wings above,
away from plans and games;
keep them as treasure in your grove,
away from evil aims.

Lord, you are blessed, O Lord Most High,
for grace to me, my liege,
working your wonders as I lie,
a city under siege.
As for my hope, in my dismay,
I fearfully surmise,
'All that I am is cut away
from you, and from your eyes.'

But you will hear my humble cry,
when I appeal to you.
Worship the Lord with loyal eye,
who watches me, is true,
punishing justly self-regard,
the remnant of the vain.
All those who wait upon the Lord,
be strong; take heart again.

Psalm 32
87 87 77
All Saints

Blessed the one who is forgiven,
whose offence is set at nought,
whose iniquity is driven
from the Lord, and out of thought,
in whose mind there is no lie,
no deceit or evil eye.

While my weary bones were silent,
through my groaning all day long;
day and night I was defiant,
when your heavy hand was strong,
sap within was dried away,
like an arid summer day.

I declared my violation,
and did not conceal my sin.
I decided on an action,
to confess my guilt within.
You forgave my sinful ways,
guilty past, and evil days.

Faithful ones will rise to pray you,
in the time of their distress.
Floods and waters never sway you,
as you guard me through the test,
you, my rock and hiding place,
where we ever sing your praise.

'Pay attention; I will teach you
in the way that you should go,
with my watchful eye to reach you,
give you counsel, make you know.
Be not like a mule or horse,
bridled, lest it range off course.'

Many pains surround the sinful,
who have never seen your face,
while the trusting, with the simple,
are surrounded by your grace.
May your saints rejoice and sing,
true of heart before their King.

Psalm 33
LM
Church Triumphant

Come, praise the Lord, you righteous choir,
with pleasing music from the lyre.
Befitting those of just repute,
come, praise the Lord upon the lute.

Play well, and sing a brand new song,
as all the upright sing along.
The Lord is true in word and deed,
his righteous love on earth decreed.

His word designed the stars in love;
his breath creating heaven above.
He poured the waters of the deep
into his treasure house to keep.

May earth approach the Lord in fear,
and all of humankind revere,
for when he spoke it came to be,
immoveable by his decree.

The Lord frustrates our human games,
he breaks in pieces cunning aims.
The counsel of the Lord is sure;
his plans are firm for evermore.

How blessed, the nation of the Lord,
who sees from heaven the earth abroad.
From his eternal throne, he views
our heart and everything we do.

The might of armies cannot save
their king or hero from the grave.
The horse's strength is bound to fall;
its power cannot redeem at all.

The Lord attends to those who fear,
who wait for kindness to appear,
to save their souls from dust and earth,
preserving them in time of dearth.

In faith we praise your holy name;
our help and shield, we will acclaim.
Lord, pour upon us all your grace,
as we rejoice to see your face.

Psalm 34 (An Alphabetic Psalm)
LM
Morning Hymn

At every time I bless the Lord;
his praise will ever be outpoured.
Because I glorify his name,
the humble hear and sing his fame.

Come, let us magnify the Lord;
as one let us exalt his word.
Down in my fears I sought his face,
and he delivered me by grace.

Emboldened by his holy name,
your faces will be clear from shame.
For, as I cried in lowly fear,
he answered, when distress was near.

God's angels camp around the just;
the Lord delivers those who trust.
How good the Lord is; taste, and see
how blessed the one that is set free.

Implore the Lord, his humble saints;
fear him, and there are no complaints.
Jejune and hungry lions fast,
but faithful folk have food to last.

Know this, you children; know the Lord;
I recommend the fear of God.
Love life and goodness every day? -
Pay heed to me, and hold his way.

Make sure your tongue does not revile,
and keep your lip from speaking guile.
Neglect the wrong, be doing good;
seek peace in every likelihood.

Observing when the righteous cry,
the Lord regards and hears on high.
Perceiving sinners and their kind,
he sees and sets them out of mind.

Responding to their contrite hearts,
he will console and take their part.
So when they cry, the Lord will hear,
to save them from distress and fear.

The righteous face tremendous pain;
the Lord will save them and sustain.
Unbroken bones he keeps secure,
for those whose faith is strong and pure.

Vexatious ones, with unjust eyes,
in hatred face an ill demise.
With spirits ransomed by the Lord,
his guiltless servants seek his word.

Psalm 35
76 76 D
Au fort de ma détresse

Lord, O contend with those, who
contend and fight with me;
battle with those who battle,
to say 'I set you free.'
Brandish a shield and buckler,
engage with those who chase;
draw forth your spear, and rise up
to help me by your grace.

Make them ashamed and humbled,
who seek to take my life;
turn them away, confounded,
who plan malicious strife.
Blow them away like ashes,
an angel driving hard;
their ways be ever slippery,
and hunted by the sword.

Laying a hidden snare, they
await without just cause,
digging a cruel ambush,
promoting unjust laws.
May devastation quickly
appear, before they know;
their very net they laid be
a fitting overthrow.

Now I delight in soul, to
rejoice before the Lord,
boasting of his salvation,
as all my bones record,
'Lord, who is like you, saving
the helpless from the strong?
You keep the unprotected
from pillaging and wrong.'

Witnesses, who are savage,
reward me ill for good,
claiming that I am guilty
of theft, as if I would.
When they were sick I fasted,
in anguish and despair.
I clothed myself in sackcloth,
but you denied my prayer.

When, as a friend or brother,
I wandered to and fro,
mourning, as for my mother,
I let my feelings show.
But, when I stumble near them,
they gather round with glee.
They strike me for no reason,
and, shouting, tear at me.

Scoffing offensive curses,
they grind me with their teeth.
How can you look, my Lord, at
unhappiness beneath?
Rescue my soul from ruin,
my darling from the maw,
to worship you in public,
and praise you evermore.

May underhanded foes, who
unjustly wink their eye,
never rejoice before me,
who twist the truth and lie.
Filling with apprehension
the quiet of the land,
they gape their mouths and bluster,
'Aha! We understand!'

You understand and see, Lord;
be not so far away.
Rise and awake from silence,
to judge my plea today.
Judge me in my contention,
according to the right,
my Lord and God, to stop them
rejoicing at my plight.

May they not say in private,
'Aha! We have *him* now!'
May they not say, '*His* soul we
will swallow anyhow!'
Make them ashamed together,
bewildered, who delight
in gloating at my trouble;
may they wear shame and slight.

Give them a ringing cry, who
delight in just redress;
may they exult together,
and endlessly confess:
'We will adore the Lord, who
delights in peaceful ways.'
Reflecting on your justice,
I praise you all my days.

Psalm 36
LM
Breslau

An evil word lurks deep inside
the wicked heart, to mesmerise.
There is no awe of God within,
no fear at all before their eyes.

For they believe their ways are smooth,
and veiled from those who hate offence.
Their words are treacherous, full of grief;
their evil plans have no defence.

They lie awake and scheme at night,
to cause anxiety and pain.
They run their course in no good way,
they do not shun a wicked strain.

O Lord, your kindness fills the sky;
your constant love is heaven's bliss,
your justice like the hill of God,
and fathoming the great abyss.

O God, you save all life on earth,
how dear your loving mercy, Lord.
Humanity, beneath your wings,
seek refuge all with one accord.

They shall be fully satisfied,
with goodness from your holy height;
you give them drink to quench their thirst,
with torrents of your sweet delight.

From you there flows a spring of life,
and in your light shall we see light.
For those who know you keep your grace,
your truth for all whose ways are right.

Let not the foot of pride control,
or wicked power offend our eyes.
There are they fallen, every foe,
thrust down and nevermore to rise.

Psalm 37 (An Alphabetic Psalm)
10 10 10 10
Anima Christi, Song 4

Always abstain from anger at your foes;
do not be jealous when injustice shows.
For, as a flower, evils fade away,
and, as the grasses, wither and decay.

Better is goodness, trusting in the Lord;
constantly dwell, and feed upon his word.
Take your delight in him and in his right;
then he will give you all your heart's delight.

Channel your way toward the Lord your God;
trust him, and he will labour for your good,
bringing your constant righteousness to light,
keeping, as noon, your faithfulness in sight.

Deep in your heart be still before the Lord;
patiently wait for him with one accord.
Do not be angry at the well-to-do,
or at the foes who plan to trouble you.

Ease off from anger and abandon ire;
let them not burn, or they may lead to fire.
Those who do evil will be cut away;
those who await their Lord will ever stay.

Folk who are evil soon will be displaced;
never returning, they will be disgraced.
Then shall the poor possess the land at ease;
they will enjoy tranquility and peace.

Guilt lies with those who plot against the just,
grinding their teeth at them in their disgust.
Then shall the Lord despise them and deride,
knowing his judgement cannot be denied.

Holding their sword and bow, the wicked draw,
ready to kill the upright and the poor.
Their very sword will thrust into their heart,
and all their bows shall break and fall apart.

If for the just there is a little good,
this is far better than a wicked brood.
Arms of the wicked break, with all their horde,
while all the righteous lean upon the Lord.

Just as the Lord knows who are good and pure,
so their possession stays for evermore.
When times are evil, they are free from ill;
when there is famine, they enjoy their fill.

Killed are the wicked, perishing like lambs;
foes of the Lord are like the fat of rams,
totally burned, cremated in the smoke,
totally burned and cut off at a stroke.

Laden with debt, the wicked never rest,
while all the righteous graciously invest.
Those who are blessed inherit through the land;
those who are cursed are cut off out of hand.

Marking our steps, the Lord will keep secure
folk he delights in, all whose ways are sure;
though they may fall, they will not touch the ground,
for he supports them, with his arm around.

Never before were righteous folk forlorn,
nor into hardship were their children born.
All day they lend, they give with generous hand,
while they are blessed with children in the land.

One who is good and shuns an evil word,
stays safe forever, faithful to the Lord.
Loving the just, the Lord will not disown,
so they are kept forever as his own.

Pestered and hounded, lawless folk are prey;
wicked descendants will be cut away.
Only the righteous may possess the land,
dwell there forever, safely in his hand.

Reason is uttered when the righteous speak,
justice and judgement forming their critique.
Statutes of God are written on their soul,
so they may never slip or lose control.

Searching, the wicked spy upon the just,
seeking to kill and satisfy their lust.
God never leaves the righteous in their power,
freeing the faithful in the judgement hour.

Trust in the Lord, and keep within his way,
so you will see the wicked cut away.
Then he will raise you up, and you will stand,
safe in possession of the promised land.

Unctuous and stretching richly like a tree,
these were the ruthless, spreading out and free.
But, when I looked, they were no longer there;
searching, I could not find them anywhere.

Virtue and blamelessness - to these attend,
for they will bring you peace until the end.
Sinners will all be massacred as one,
wicked descendants ever are undone.

When, from the Lord, the righteous find release,
during their need, salvation comes in peace.
He will protect them, save them from the foe,
when they seek refuge in the God they know.

Psalm 38
65 65
Caswall

Lord, do not reprove me
in your wrath and ire;
do not scourge and scold me
with your angry fire.

For you wound and pierce with
arrow, barb and dart,
while your hand descends and
weighs upon my heart.

All my flesh is feeble
from your wrath within;
every bone is weak by
reason of my sin.

My mistakes and guilt have
passed above my head,
like a heavy burden,
heavier than lead.

Stinking putrefaction
oozes from my sores,
as my senseless folly
leaches through my pores.

I am doubled over,
bowed and bending low,
as I wander round all
day with darkened brow.

For my loins are filled with
constant burning pain,
as my flesh is failing,
weakened by the strain.

I am numb and listless,
crushed and blown away,
while I roar in pain, and
groan in my dismay.

All my hope and longing
lie before you, Lord;
you can see my sighing,
taking it onboard.

Now my strength is failing;
panic strikes my mind;
losing light and vision,
I am going blind.

Neighbours have departed,
fearing my disease;
dearest friends are distant,
heedless to my pleas.

Striking hard, they hurt me
to achieve their goal;
constantly they plan and
seek to catch my soul.

I am like the deaf who
cannot hear a sound,
I am like the dumb whose
tongue is ever bound.

I am like the one who
cannot hear a sound,
who has no defence to
silence or confound.

So to you, my hope, I
look for my reward,
you alone can answer,
you, my God and Lord.

I have said, 'O let them
not enjoy my gall,
vaunt themselves against me,
when I slip and fall.'

I am ready now to
stumble on the ground;
constantly beside me
are my pain and wound.

For I will declare my
wickedness within;
I am very anxious,
knowing all my sin.

All my foes are mighty,
full of life and strong,
many now who hate me,
though I do no wrong.

Enemies reward me
evil deeds for good,
while I work to follow
everything I should.

Lord, do not forsake me;
hear me in my need.
God, be not so distant,
heedless, as I plead.

Hasten now to help me
when I am afraid.
Lord, be my salvation;
hurry to my aid.

Psalm 39
DCM
Third Mode Melody

I said that I would keep my ways,
in case my tongue should sin,
defend my mouth from wicked folk,
restrained and still within.
In silence searing pain was stirred;
my indignation flared.
I murmured, while the fury burned,
and then my tongue declared:

'Lord, let me know my end and fate,
how long I have to live.
To you my mortal days abate,
no matter how I strive.'
For humankind is mist and smoke;
we walk about in gloom.
We toil and work, not knowing who
will place us in the tomb.

Why do I wait? What is my hope?
My Lord, you are my goal.
O make me not a laughing-stock;
from sin release my soul.
For I have bound and shut my mouth,
O take your plague away,
your angry and contentious hand;
I am undone today.

You chasten us, rebuke our sin;
the moth consumes our lust.
Humanity is mist and smoke;
our forebears pass to dust.
Lord, hear my prayer, consider well
a traveller's cry and tears,
and look away that I may smile,
before I meet the years.

Psalm 40
DCM
Christmas Carol (Walford Davies)

I gladly waited here for God;
he quickly turned his ear.
From roaring pit and miry sod
he drew me from my fear.
Upon his rock he placed my feet,
established and secure,
and, with a new song to repeat,
his praise has made me sure.

Then those who see will fear the Lord,
who fosters trust within.
Blessed is the one who trusts his word,
who does not turn to sin,
who does not trust in foolish pride,
or err with those who lie,
who keeps you near to lead and guide,
and trusts wholeheartedly.

My Lord and God, how many are
the wonders you have done!
You comprehend us from afar,
who live beneath the sun.
Your wonders and your thoughts to us
can never be compared.
Were I to count them or discuss,
they could not be declared.

You have not asked for sacrifice,
instead an open ear,
in place of holocaust or spice
I answered, 'I am here!'
According to the written scroll,
I long to do your will.
Your law is hidden in my soul,
and gently guides me still.

Your righteousness was on my tongue;
I spoke for all to hear,
did not restrain my lips, among
the faithful who revere.
I did not hide your truth and grace,
your victory far away,
from any who approach your face,
to worship you and pray.

My Lord, do not withhold your grace
from all my guilt and sin,
for untold evils, set in place,
have caught my soul within.
May truth and mercy be my shield,
for I no longer see.
My countless wrongs have been revealed;
my heart is failing me.

My Lord, be pleased to rescue me;
my Lord, give aid today.
Let them be shamed, who all agree
to sweep my soul away.
Let them be driven and debased,
who long for my demise.
Let them be ruined and disgraced,
who hurl abusive cries.

Let them exult and celebrate,
who seek you and confess.
Let them declare, 'The Lord is great!'
who love your righteousness.
While I am poor and full of strife,
Lord, hear my prayer today.
You give me help and save my life;
my God, do not delay.

Psalm 41

11 10 11 10 11 10 11 12
Londonderry Air

Blessed are the ones who pay heed to the needy;
the Lord will save them in an evil day;
preserving lives, the Lord delivers freely;
they shall be blessed at home and far away.
You will not hand them over to the fervour
of bitter foes, who counter and complain;
and on their sickbed you are their preserver;
the Lord will overturn their deadly bed of pain.

But as for me, I said, 'O Lord, be gracious,
to heal my life; against you I have sinned.'
While speaking ill, my rivals are rapacious:
'When shall *he* perish and *his* lamp be dimmed?'
And if they come to see me they are hollow,
reciting fair, their hearts amassing foul;
so when they leave they speak to those who follow,
arousing discontent against my heart and soul.

All those who hate me congregate against me;
they whisper, '*He* is nearly good as dead:
for there is deadly poison in *his* body;
he cannot live or get up from *his* bed.'
Yes, even one who was my close companion,
the one I trusted and who ate my bread,
has turned against me, boasting with abandon,
rejecting love and choosing wickedness instead.

But you, O Lord, be gracious and restore me,
and I will pay them back for all their ill.
By this I know your favour is before me:
the hateful cries of enemies are still.
For you uphold my honour and endeavour,
you place me, safe before you once again.
The Lord and God of Israel is for ever,
and blessed from evermore to evermore. Amen.

Psalm 42
SM
Trentham

As when the running deer
longs for a flowing stream,
so my soul longs for you, O God,
to save and to redeem.

I am athirst for God,
giver of life and grace.
When shall I come before my God,
or stand before his face?

Tears are my only bread,
day and night overawed,
and all day long they say to me,
'So where is he, your God?'

These things I call to mind,
when I pour out my soul,
and, with the multitude, I pass,
as I approach my goal.

Leading the festal throng
into the house of God,
ringing my joy, I dance and sing,
as they adore the Lord.

Why so cast down, my soul?
Why murmur in despair?
Wait on your God! I praise the one,
who saves, and hears my prayer.

God, I am so cast down,
as I remember you;
Jordan surrounds, and Hermon's peaks,
with Mizar, fill my view.

Deep calls to endless deep,
thundering tracts beneath;
over my head your breakers pass
their waves and waves of death.

Lord, you are good by day,
sending me grace in strife;
music from you becomes, at night,
a prayer to God, my life.

I will address my rock,
'Why must I walk in shade?
Why have you quite forgotten me,
as foes oppress and raid?'

Feeble and shattered bones,
foes who reproach and nod,
and all day long they say to me,
'So where is he, your God?'

Why so cast down, my soul?
Why murmur in despair?
Wait on your God! I praise the one,
who saves, and hears my prayer.

Psalm 43
SM
Trentham

Save me, O God my God;
judge me and plead my case,
stop their injustice, their deceit,
when they abandon grace.

You are my God, my rock.
Why must I walk in shade?
Why have you quite rejected me,
as foes oppress and raid?

Send out your light and truth;
send them to lead me hence,
bring me to see your sacred hill,
approach your holy tents.

Let me approach your shrine,
come to my great delight,
praise you with music on the lyre,
O God, my God and light.

Why so cast down, my soul?
Why murmur in despair?
Wait on your God! I praise the one,
who saves, and hears my prayer.

Psalm 44
7676 D
King's Lynn

Our forebears, God, have told us,
our ears have heard your ways;
your deeds unfold before us,
your work of former days.
You dispossessed the nations,
and planted us to stay,
afflicted all their stations,
and drove them all away.

Their sword was not their strength, when
they dispossessed the land,
nor did their own arm save them,
but your right arm and hand,
your glory and your presence,
the sign of your delight.
My King and God, your sentence
was victory and light.

By you our foes were scattered;
we trampled them to dust.
My sword was not what mattered;
my bow was not my trust.
You offered us salvation,
you shamed the hateful foe.
In God our celebration
would ever overflow.

But you reject and shame us;
you disregard our corps;
you turn us back and maim us,
defeated in the war.
As sheep with no remittance,
you scatter us away;
you sell us for a pittance,
the bargain of the day.

My insult is before me,
a never-ending shame;
the enemy abhor me,
reproach and curse my name,
insulted by the peoples,
derided and disdained.
They sneer at all our evils;
our name has been profaned.

All this has come upon us,
yet we remembered you.
Your covenant is still with us,
and we are ever true.
We have not been unjust, as
we have not gone astray.
With demons you have crushed us,
in dark and death today.

If we had not remembered
the honour of our God,
if we had all surrendered
to deities abroad,
would you have not considered,
who know the secret heart,
for whom we are disfigured,
as sheep, and torn apart?

Wake up! Why are you sleeping,
rejecting us so long,
and why are you ignoring
their pillaging and wrong?
Awake! Look down to see us,
with dirt upon our face.
Arise to help and free us,
O call to mind your grace.

Psalm 45
11 10 11 10
O Perfect Love, Strength and Stay

Here, as my heart stirs eloquence within me,
I will recite my work before the king.
So now my tongue pens poetry, to win me
thanks from his throne, as I perform and sing.

Perfect and charming, more than any creature,
grace has been poured upon you at your door.
Beauty is yours, divine in every feature;
wherefore your God has blessed you evermore.

Gird on your sword and belt, you mighty warrior,
glorious in splendour, dignity and fame.
Ride on in truth to conquer every barrier,
fighting for right, your true and humble name.

May your right hand impose a fearful lesson;
arrows will pierce the folk who disobey,
foes who rise up in hate to plot aggression,
peoples who perish, as they flee away.

Righteous, your throne will stand, O God, forever,
sceptre of royal name and noble ends.
Yearning for justice, hating your oppressor,
God has anointed you above your friends.

Fragrant with spices, splendid robes commend you,
music from palaces your sweet delight.
Princesses stand with ladies who attend you;
gorgeous in gold, the queen is at your right.

Daughter, O hear me; look towards the future,
leaving your people and your father's house.
Worship the king, for he, your lord and ruler,
longs for your beauty as his loving spouse.

Daughters from Tyre shall seek you with a present -
riches and treasure, glorious to behold.
Within her room our princess is resplendent,
wearing a gorgeous dress of finest gold.

Brought to the king, with virgins who attend her,
lavishly dressed, she is a stunning sight.
Maidens behind, to usher and commend her,
enter the palaces with great delight.

Children console you for the loss of parents;
they will be princes to the furthest shore.
Then, as your name resounds in their descendants,
peoples will offer praises evermore.

Psalm 46
76 76 D and Refrain
Wir Pflügen

Our God is our defender,
our castle and our keep.
We will not fear the earthquake,
the roaring of the deep,
the dark and rolling mountains,
the boiling, angry foam,
the waters of the ocean
in their eternal home.

God Most High is with us,
the Lord of Hosts is here,
the God of Jacob is our rock
from year to year.

Within the holy city
there flows a living stream,
and God Most High resides there,
to help her and redeem.
The nations boil in anger,
in rage the kingdoms foam.
Your voice will melt creation
from your eternal home.

God Most High is with us,
the Lord of Hosts is here,
the God of Jacob is our rock
from year to year.

So come to see the Lord, who
will devastate the earth.
Removing war and conflict,
he brings his peace to birth,
destroying bows and lances,
their military might.
'Be still and know my name, as
I rise up in their sight.'

God Most High is with us,
the Lord of Hosts is here,
the God of Jacob is our rock
from year to year.

Psalm 47
LM
Deus Tuorum Militum

All peoples, clap your hands on high,
and shout to God with ringing cry;
the Lord, Most High above, is feared,
as King of all the earth revered.

Our God subdues, beneath our feet,
the scattered peoples in defeat,
who chooses our possession here,
the pride of Jacob, ever dear.

The Lord ascends, with trumpet call
and horn, into his holy hall.
Give praise to God, give praise and sing,
give praises to our heavenly King.

For God is King of all the earth;
give praise and sing, proclaim his worth,
who reigns on high in every state,
enthroned as Lord and magistrate.

The nobles of the peoples now
acknowledge God, and, bending low,
they are a single tribe and clan,
to raise the God of Abraham.

Psalm 48
65 65 D and Refrain
St. Gertrude

God is great in Zion,
highly to be praised,
on the sacred mountain,
elegant and raised,
in the royal city,
fortified for war;
God is her defence, and
guards her evermore.

*We have heard the rumour
and confirm the word.
This is God's own city,
armies of the Lord!*

Kings arose together,
swept across to fight.
They were overwhelmed and
staggered at the sight,
filled with fear and trembling,
writhing in defeat,
reeling, as your tempest
burst upon their fleet.

*We have heard the rumour
and confirm the word.
This is God's own city,
armies of the Lord!*

In your temple courts we
re-enact your grace.
God, your name is praised in
every time and place,
justice in your right hand,
judgements in your voice.
Now let Zion sing, and
Judah's towns rejoice.

We have heard the rumour
and confirm the word.
This is God's own city,
armies of the Lord!

Wander through Mount Zion,
count her many towers,
lay to heart her ramparts,
scrutinise her powers.
Tell it to your children,
when our days are gone,
'God is ours for ever,
and will lead us on.'

We have heard the rumour
and confirm the word.
This is God's own city,
armies of the Lord!

Psalm 49
13 13 13 13 13 13
Thaxted

O hear this, every people,
and listen to my word;
you children of creation,
come, let my song be heard;
you rich and poor together,
of great or little worth:
I speak with understanding,
and contemplate the earth.
Unfolding my conundrum,
my riddle to the lyre,
my mouth will utter insight,
my spirit will inspire.

O why should I be frightened
of evil at my door,
of brutes who overpower,
or trust in all their store?
They boast of all their riches,
they boast of all their wealth,
but treasure cannot save them,
or keep them in good health.
Their souls cannot be bought, or
eternally secured.
We cannot live forever;
our death is well assured.

Yes, we can all be certain
that death awaits us all;
the wise and fool together
eventually will fall.
They leave their wealth to others,
with all their grand estate;
their home will be the graveyard,
where generations wait.
The rich who never ponder,
who do not understand,
are simpleminded oxen,
that perish out of hand.

Their ways are superficial,
self-satisfied and blind,
and, like a sheep for slaughter,
they follow on behind;
with Sheol for their shepherd,
descending to the grave,
corruption is their fortress,
to capture and enslave.
But God is my redeemer;
he will release my soul,
he saves me from the power
of Sheol's dark control.

So, do not fear the rich, or
their splendour and increase,
for nothing stays forever,
no glory in decease.
Although they bless themselves, and
you also in your might,
their souls descend to shadow,
and, hidden from the light,
the rich who never ponder,
who do not understand,
are simpleminded oxen,
that perish out of hand.

Psalm 50

11 11 11 11
St. Denio

The Lord of the ages, the Father of Years,
from Zion, perfection of beauty, appears.
He summons the earth, from the south to the north;
from sunrise to sunset his splendour shines forth.

Our God, who is coming in lightning and storm,
will never be silent, with burning reform;
he summons the heavens and, calling the world,
administers justice, his judgement unfurled.

'Come, gather together the faithful, who heard,
who sealed an agreement, and gave me their word.
The heavens are telling my honour and might,
for I am your God, who loves justice and right.

'Now hear me, you people, the whole human race.
To you, and to Israel, I set out my case;
for I am your true God, the only one here,
eternal and mighty, the God you should fear.

'I will not reprove you for gifts you have made;
your vows and oblations have fully been paid.
I do not require any bull from the field,
or ram from the pasture, a tenth of the yield.

'The beasts of the forest, and cattle, are mine;
the sheep and the oxen are there by design;
I know all the birds as they circle around;
I know every insect that crawls on the ground.

'If I became hungry, I would not tell you;
the world and its fullness is all in my view.
So how can you think that I make myself full,
with blood from a goat, or with flesh from a bull?

'Your offering to me should be blessing and prayer;
to God the Most High pay the vows that you swear.
Then raise your appeal in the day of distress,
and glorify God, when I save you, and bless.

'But why are the wicked reciting my laws,
or quoting my covenant, each statute and clause?
You hate my rebuke, and you wander astray;
you take my commandments, and throw them away.

'If you saw a thief, you would follow along;
in your eyes adulterers have done nothing wrong.
Your mouth pours out evil, and, filled with conceit,
your tongue is offensive, contriving deceit.

'You sit there and smear your own sibling with lies;
you slander your family, the kin you despise.
When I held my peace, you thought I was like you,
but I will condemn you; my judgements are true.

'Let those who forget me beware and behave,
in case I devour you, with no-one to save.
Your gift of thanksgiving increases my praise;
deliverance is yours, if you follow my ways.'

Psalm 51
11 11 11 5
Herzliebster Jesu

My God, be gracious, show consideration,
according to your kindness and affection.
According to the wealth of your compassion,
clear my transgression.

Completely wash away my great offences,
and cleanse me from their fitting consequences.
For truly my transgressions, yes, I see them.
I cannot flee them.

Against you only is my sin directed,
and in your sight my guilt is all collected.
You will be just and pure in bringing vengeance,
when you pass sentence.

From birth my guilt has ever been beside me;
conceived in sin, I nurture it inside me.
But you delight in honesty and vision,
your hidden wisdom.

With hyssop purge me, symbol of forgiveness,
and wash me, white as snow, to make me sinless.
May shattered bones rejoice with exaltation
and jubilation.

Ignore my anger, my unjust aggression;
O wipe away my error and transgression.
Establish and renew my soul to guide me,
clean heart inside me.

Do not dismiss me from your side to break me,
nor let your holy spirit quite forsake me.
Bring back to me your noble inspiration,
joyful salvation.

I teach your righteous ways among the lawless,
so they return to you, becoming flawless.
O save me, God, from bloodshed and from malice,
to sing your justice.

Lord, open now my lips that I may sing you,
with heart and mouth and perfect praise to bring you.
You take no pleasure in exotic spices,
no sacrifices.

Instead of sacrifice and reparation,
I bring my guilty soul as my oblation.
My crushed and broken heart, my broken spirit,
you will receive it.

Do good to Zion in your grace and pity;
rebuild Jerusalem, your holy city.
Then they will offer bulls upon your altar,
with song and psalter.

Psalm 52
CM
St. Nicholas (Greene)

Why do you boast, you mighty one,
of evil all the day?
God, who is Father of the Years,
is kind in every way.

Look how your tongue contrives deceit,
with razor-sharp delight,
loving the evil more than good,
deception more than right.

Look how you swallow up the truth,
with cunning and pretence.
Oh yes! The Father of the Years
will tear you from your tent.

When he uproots you from the land,
your life before our face,
then will the righteous laugh, to see
and hear of your disgrace.

You thought that God would never be
protection you could trust.
You looked for safety in your wealth,
and overweening lust.

I, though, am like an olive tree,
within the sacred grove,
trusting in God for evermore,
his mercy, grace and love.

So I will praise you for your deeds,
as days and years ensue,
waiting upon your blessed name,
with those who worship you.

Psalm 53
887
Stabat Mater

Fools deny their God within them,
while they work unrighteous mayhem;
there is no-one virtuous.

Then our God from heaven descended,
and our nature comprehended:
was there thought or thirst for God?

All have gone astray together,
fraudulent in their endeavour,
no-one upright here at all.

Wicked-doers have no knowledge,
as they swallow those in bondage.
They do not proclaim their God.

All the wicked shall be daunted,
and by fear and terror haunted,
shattered bones and empty camps.

You, my God, have scorned the vicious,
and their cruel, vain, ambitious
plans; you have rejected them.

Who will give relief from Zion,
freeing captives from their prison?
May his people all rejoice!

Psalm 54
SM
St. Paul's (Stainer)

God, save me by your name,
and judge me by your might.
God, hear my prayer, and may my word
be spoken in your sight.

The insolent rise up;
the ruthless seek my soul.
They have not set their heart on God,
or bowed to your control.

But God will be my help;
the Lord sustains my breath.
May evil fall on those who plot,
and truth put them to death.

I make an offering now,
a gift of my free will.
I praise your name, for it is good;
O Lord, I praise you still.

For you will save my soul
from all of my distress.
My eye looks down upon my foes,
and boasts of your success.

Psalm 55

77 77 77
Petra (Redhead No. 76)

Listen, God, with sympathy;
do not disregard my plea.
I am restless and appalled,
cannot concentrate at all.
Pay attention, God, to hear
my confusion and my fear.

I can see my enemy,
as they try to pressure me,
how they cherish rage and spite,
troubling me in great delight.
They abuse with angry face,
tainting me with their disgrace.

As my heart and soul recoil,
blasphemy and curse embroil,
deadly terrors overpower,
nervous tension every hour.
Now convulsions cover me,
ever trembling - hear my plea:

'How I wish that I could fly,
like a dove, from stress and sigh,
find a desert place to stay,
growing wings to soar away!'
I would quickly disappear,
from their storm and tempest here.

In a city full of sin,
violence, wrath and strife within,
constant grinding toil and pain,
lust, abuse and lies remain.
Day and night their tongues resound;
tear them, Lord, and bring them down.

There was not a foe to see,
boasting or reproaching me.
Willingly I could endure
one who hated me for sure.
But - I cannot comprehend -
it was you, my own dear friend.

[Even though I treasured you,
loved your counsel through and through,
even though we walked along,
in the temple, with the throng,
may your death come quickly now;
may you go to hell below.]

Sin and evil permeate
their intention and estate.
I will call to God, my Lord,
to protect me with a word.
Day and night I cry again,
so that God may know my pain.

He redeems my soul today,
making conflict pass away.
He, the Father of the Years,
terrifies, as he appears,
those at ease and ever still,
all who do not fear his will.

Broken covenants, evil ends,
wicked folk, betraying friends,
nursing warfare in their heart,
spreading words with easy art,
though their speech is soft as oil,
it will cut, a brandished foil.

Cast your burden on the Lord;
God will be your stay and ward.
he will keep the righteous fast;
lies and bloodshed never last.
Bring them down, their days be few!
As for me, I trust in you.

Psalm 56
86 88 6
Repton

O God, in mercy look to me,
for I am trampled low.
All day they challenge me and fight,
oppressors watch me from their height,
to strike and overthrow,
to strike and overthrow.

When I am nervous and afraid,
I trust in your decree.
In God, the Lord, whose word is dear,
in God I trust, and will not fear.
What can they do to me?
What can they do to me?

All day they falsify my words,
with evil schemes and strife,
while secretly they trail and track,
they keep a watch behind my back,
to take away my life,
to take away my life.

Will they escape their wickedness,
who wait to snare my soul?
You count my wanderings as I pass,
decant my tears into your glass;
you note them in a scroll,
you note them in a scroll.

Bring down my foes in wrath, O God,
confirming your decree.
In God, the Lord, whose word is dear,
in God I trust, and will not fear.
What can they do to me?
What can they do to me?

I call to you, and then my foes
withdraw in disarray,
for God is with me, this I know.
I pay in full the vows I owe,
my sacrifice today,
my sacrifice today.

For you deliver me from death;
my feet are sound and shod.
I will not stumble during strife,
but follow you, the light of life,
to walk before my God,
to walk before my God.

Psalm 57
LM
Deus Tuorum Militum

Be gracious, God, and rescue me;
to you I look for sanctuary,
beneath your wings and gracious eye,
until destruction passes by.

To God Most High I make my prayer;
O God, you keep me in your care.
You send from heaven to save my soul,
reproaching those who tramp and troll.

O God, send forth your loving grace,
with truth and mercy from your face,
among the lions where I lie,
the folk who roar and blaze near by.

They utter barbs with every word;
their tongue is like a sharpened sword.
O God, let heaven proclaim your worth,
your glory over all the earth.

Beneath my feet they set a snare:
my soul is shrinking in despair.
The pit they dug before my face
will be their final resting place.

O God, my heart will ever sing,
give praise and music to my King.
With lute and harp awake, to play
the glorious music of the day!

I praise the Lord with heart and voice;
among the peoples I rejoice,
to offer music for my King;
may all the nations hear me sing.

The heavenly powers magnify
your truth and grace, above the sky.
O God, let heaven proclaim your worth,
your glory over all the earth.

Psalm 58

10 10 10 10 10 10
Eddleston, Finlandia

[Do you, O gods, declare in righteousness?
Is there integrity in your regime?
Do you, O leaders, judge with even hand,
or try in equity the evil scheme?
Oh no! You bring unlawfulness to birth,
apportion violence all across the earth.

Even from birth the wicked are estranged;
lying and uttering falsehood from the womb.
Venom is theirs, the venom of a snake,
an adder's poison burning in the gloom,
a cobra, deaf and totally immune
to curse or spell or whispered, mystic rune.

Break now their teeth, O God, within their mouths.
Tear out the fangs of lions by your word.
Like water pour them out upon the ground,
your arrows flying straight to kill them, Lord.
Like slugs let them dissolve and melt away,
like foetuses that never see the day.

Like dust the Lord will sweep them all away,
thorny and crackling brambles in the fire.
Then will the righteous vengefully rejoice,
and wash their feet in wicked blood and ire.
So they will say, 'At last our God above
is judging earth in righteousness and love!']

Psalm 59
10 10 10 10
Ellers

Save me, my God, from every hateful foe,
raise me above all those who take their stand.
Save me from wickedness and overthrow,
from those who stir up bloodshed in the land.

Look how they lie in ambush for my soul,
using their strength to battle and contest;
nothing against me, Lord, is in your scroll;
there is no sin, for which I am oppressed.

Rise up, O Lord, to meet me and enquire;
visit the nations, God of Hosts, to see.
You, God of Israel, you condemn the liar,
those who are working ill, and troubling me.

Dogs on the prowl, at evening they appear,
growling around our city in the night.
Swords are their lips, insulting as they sneer,
'For who,' they say, 'will listen to indict?'

You, though, my Lord, will treat them with disdain,
spurning the nations gathered at your feet.
You are my strength; I watch for you to reign,
since you are God, and you are my retreat.

God, in your kindness aid us and abet;
show me the folk who seek to overthrow.
Do not destroy them, lest we all forget;
fill them with terror, come and bring them low.

[Note all their sin, my Lord and our defence;
let them be seized and taken in their pride.
Think of their lies and blasphemous offence;
may there be nowhere left for them to hide.

Finish them off, abolish in disdain;
totally wipe them from the earth in rage.
Then they will know there is a God who reigns,
ruling from Jacob every human stage.]

Dogs on the prowl, at evening they return,
growling around our city in the night.
Wandering about for food at every turn,
and, if not satisfied, they snarl and bite.

But, as for me, I praise your might and power;
ring out your love as morning brings the day.
You are my fortress, you my sturdy tower,
refuge in trouble, every time I pray.

You are my strength; to you I make my song.
You are my God, my fortress and my height.
You are my God, and so to you belong
mercy and love, my God and great delight.

Psalm 60
LM
Deus Tuorum Militum

O God, you have rejected us;
reversals have afflicted us.
Your anger broke across the land;
return with love and mighty hand.

The quaking earth, beneath our feet,
was breaking open in defeat;
We stagger badly in the war;
revive us now; O God, restore.

For you have shown yourself severe;
you give us wine, and, drunk with fear,
the folk who fear you flee away
from war, in total disarray.

O God, arise, deliver now,
and save your treasure here below.
Establish us, and give to me
an answer from your sanctuary.

'The land of Shechem I divide,
I measure Sukkoth in my pride.
Manasseh, Gilead - they are mine,
with Ephraim on my head to shine.

The land of Judah is a staff;
at Edom, Moab, I will laugh.
The Philistines will be afraid,
as I, with victory shout, invade.'

Will you, O God, engage the siege
of Edom, and invade the breach?
For you have left us on our own;
our armies go to war alone.

O be our saviour once again,
for human armies march in vain.
In God the soldiers overthrow,
for you will trample down the foe.

Psalm 61
LM
O Waly Waly

God, hear my ringing cry and care;
O turn your ear towards my prayer.
From endless exile, my complaint
will rise to you, when I am faint.

Then you will guide me to your height,
a rock above and out of sight.
For you have been my place to go,
a stronghold from my hateful foe.

So I will dwell within your tent,
for years and years with your consent,
and look for safety, Lord of kings,
beneath the covering of your wings.

For you, O God, have heard my pledge;
you give to me my home and hedge,
estate of grace, for those who fear
your holy name, who worship here.

The king will live, and, from your store,
prolong his days for evermore,
to sit enthroned for years on earth,
as generations come to birth.

May love and truth around him stand,
a royal guard at his right hand.
And as I sing your holy name,
I pay my vows, each day the same.

Psalm 62
664 6664
Olivet

Father, I wait for you,
quiet, I wait for you,
safe and secure.
God is a trusty rock,
fortress and sturdy lock,
saving me from the shock,
protected, sure.

Why do you threaten me,
challenge my dignity?
You shall be slain.
They are a leaning wall,
swaying and bound to fall;
falsely they bless, and all
they say is vain.

So I will wait for God,
quiet, I hope for God,
safe and secure.
God is a trusty rock,
fortress and sturdy lock,
saving me from the shock,
protected, sure.

God is a strength to me,
fortress and sanctuary,
glory and power.
People of every race,
constantly plead for grace;
God will, in every case,
remain their tower.

People are vanity,
lying humanity,
flying away.
Trust not in robbery,
vigour or snobbery;
wealth turns to poverty,
and does not pay.

One thing God said to me,
twice he has read to me:
strength comes from God.
Grace is from you, my Lord,
and, by your holy word,
you give what we deserve
beneath your rod.

Psalm 63
10 10 10 10 10 10
Song 1

My God, I look to you with longing eyes;
my soul is parched and thirsting for your face;
my flesh is faint, consumed by fears and sighs,
a desert land, bereft of life and grace.
I yearn and look towards the sacred height,
to see the glorious vision of your might.

Your love and grace refresh me and revive;
my lips will praise you time and time again.
And so I bless you, while I am alive,
lift up my hands to sing your holy name.
My soul enjoys the marrow and the cream;
my lips ring out their praise and joyful theme.

Upon my bed I ponder in the night,
as I recall your presence is near by.
For you have been my helper and my light;
beneath your wings I make my ringing cry.
My soul clings onto you with every breath;
your right hand holds me up, in life and death.

[Then those who seek my soul will go to hell,
beneath the earth to hidden depths below,
and, butchered by the sword when they rebel,
they lie on open ground with every foe.
The king, and those who swear by God, will praise,
rejoicing as you end all lying ways.]

Psalm 64
77 77
Aus der Tiefe (Heinlein)

Hear me, God, when I complain;
guard me from the hateful foe.
Hide me from an evil strain,
crowds who trouble me below.

Tongues and words are sharp as swords,
bitter arrows all arrayed,
shooting stealthily towards
honest people, unafraid.

Secretly they all conspire;
they discuss their evil snares,
satisfied that their desire
goes unseen, their foul affairs.

Though their thoughts may be profound,
God will shoot them and will slay.
Swiftly, as their words rebound,
they will flee in disarray.

So humanity will fear;
all will openly declare,
that the Lord is really near,
working wonders everywhere.

Then the righteous will rejoice,
seeking refuge in the Lord;
then the just will raise their voice,
praising God with one accord.

Psalm 65
87 87 D
Blaenwern

Human praise is dumb before you,
Lord our God, in Zion's place.
We fulfil the vows we swore you;
prayers are answered by your grace.
All the human race approaches,
burdened by their sin and crime,
overpowered by our reproaches;
you forgive us all the time.

When you bring the chosen near you,
to reside within your court,
we are sated, and revere you,
filled with good of every sort.
You respond with fearful justice,
saving by your powerful hand,
Faith in you, and lasting trust, is
far and wide, in distant lands.

You created mountain ranges,
by your strength, their hidden caves,
stilled the furious ocean rages,
calmed the roaring of their waves.
While the hordes of distant races
fear your wonders in the sky,
day and evening, from their places,
offer up their ringing cry.

Visit earth with endless riches,
making food and goodness grow;
drench the furrows, fill the ditches,
as your treasuries overflow,
softening all the land with showers,
filling rivers in your love;
bless the corn with fruit and flowers,
milk and honey from above.

Crown the seasons with your goodness,
pouring down from your parade:
desert pastures, in their fulness,
hill and vale and field arrayed,
full of sheep and joy and laughter,
stores of wine and food and grain.
Now with joy, and ever after,
in your house we sing again.

Psalm 66
87 87 87
Neander (Unser Herrscher)

Sing to God, you earth, in triumph,
glorify his sacred name.
Bring to God your songs of glory,
sing his universal fame.
Say to God, 'Your deeds are glorious;
they will ever be the same.

'By the greatness of your power,
by the might of your decree,
every foe will cringe before you,
entering in on bended knee.
All the earth will bow in worship,
bring a song and melody.'

Come to see the acts of God, who
works amazing deeds on earth,
turning oceans into pathways,
bringing Israel to birth.
When they crossed the river dry shod,
we were glad and filled with mirth.

God for ever rules in power,
looking after great and small.
There cannot be proud rebellion,
no disloyalty at all.
Peoples, bless our God, and let your
praise resound in house and hall.

God, the Lord, is our salvation,
guarding souls in life and light,
keeps the erring footsteps steady,
with perpetual oversight;
he has tried us and refined us,
pure as silver, burnished bright.

When the snares are brought upon us,
when you grieve our minds with scourge,
foes arise to trample on us,
we may pass through fire and surge;
you will lead us out of trouble,
with relief as we emerge.

I will offer whole burnt offerings,
vows I made with holy word,
keep the promise made in trouble,
as my soul within was stirred:
bulls and fatlings I present you,
from the flock and from the herd.

Let the faithful pay attention,
hear what God has done for me.
I arose with lofty praises;
now my life has been set free.
Had I cherished guilt within, the
Lord would not have heard my plea.

Nonetheless my God has heard me,
paid attention to my prayer.
He received my supplication,
did not leave me in despair.
Bless our God, whose loving-kindness
lasts forever, everywhere.

Psalm 67
LM
Illsley

Be gracious, God, and bless us here;
in glory may you now appear.
Be praised in joy upon the earth,
your great salvation brought to birth.

May peoples everywhere acclaim,
and come to praise your holy name.
The races glory and rejoice
across the earth, with single voice.

For you will judge the world with right,
exhorting nations in your sight.
May peoples everywhere acclaim,
and come to praise your holy name.

We now enjoy the fruits of earth,
the gifts that you have brought to birth.
In faith may all the world revere,
and God forever bless us here.

Psalm 68
DLM
St. Patrick

Let God arise and scatter foes,
so hate and malice flee away.
Like driven smoke or melting wax,
the wicked perish back to clay.
But let the righteous sing to God
in celebration, with one voice,
exult together, sing for joy;
and let them all in heart rejoice.

Come, celebrate and sing to God;
his battle chariot flies on high.
Make music to his holy name,
to God, who drives across the sky,
the Father of the orphan child,
the widows' holy advocate,
who frees the bound, brings home the lost,
and makes the rebels desolate.

God, when you marched your people out
of Sinai, where you used to dwell,
the very earth and heavens quaked,
to see the God of Israel.
You showered down your gracious rain,
secured your people after war,
refreshed your weary heritage,
prepared in goodness for the poor.

My Lord commands the word to us,
and messengers in hosts announce,
'Their kings retreat!' and women share
the spoil at home, in vast amounts.
You lie with flocks, as doves fly in,
with glinting gold and silver wings.
Like snow on Salmon all around,
Almighty God has scattered kings.

You mount of Bashan, mount of God,
and all you northern peaks as well,
why look with envy at the hill,
where God, the Lord, is pleased to dwell?
Yes, there the Lord will ever stay,
with myriads in his chariotry,
surrounded by the heavenly host
of Sinai, to his sanctuary.

Ascending to his sacred height,
our God, the Lord, will ever dwell,
with tribute from humanity,
and captives, all who would rebel.
So blessed be God in righteousness,
and blessed, our Lord from day to day;
by God, the Lord of saving power,
may death be banished far away.

[But God will smite our hateful foes,
and all who walk in treacherous ways;
he strikes their hairy crown and head,
with butchery, in vengeful days.
The Lord our God will bring us here,
from Bashan's height and deepest sea,
to wash our feet in blood and gore,
while dogs devour the enemy.]

In great processions, God, our King,
our princes lead us at the head;
our singers follow on behind,
and girls, with timbrels, in their stead.
They bless our Lord from Israel,
with Benjamin, who leads their throng,
while princes come from Judah's clan,
from Naphtali and Zebulun.

Command your might, O God; be strong
and rule, from Zion's sacred height,
as you have done for us before;
may kings bring tribute in your sight.
Restrain the savage wetland beast,
their brutish herds and foreign hordes,
who come with silver, trampled down,
to bring before you their rewards.

Ambassadors from Egypt come
to God, with Ethiopia's might.
You turn and scatter far away
all those, who love to war and fight.
Come, sing to God, you earthly realms,
with music to our Lord on high,
who rides his clouds in heaven above,
in thunder crash across the sky.

Give strength to God, whose pride extends
in all the clouds, to Israel,
the ancient Father of the Years,
and faithful God of Israel.
Our God is feared in every place,
in holy temple, sacred height,
who gives his people strength and power.
So blessed be God, the God of might.

Psalm 69

11 11 11 5
Iste Confessor, Cloisters

Save me, O God! The waters overcome me.
Nowhere to stand, dark mire is up above me.
Sinking too deep, your tide has overrun me.
Floods overwhelm me.

I have no strength left, worn away with crying,
weary and parched, because of all my sighing.
Eyesight is failing, light is almost dying,
waiting for you, God.

How many foes are hating me unjustly,
spreading their lies, attacking me robustly!
I must return their property, so costly,
which I did not steal.

Lord God of Hosts, you understand my weakness.
Let not my failings scandalise their meekness,
those who have served you, innocent and heedless,
Lord God of Israel.

On your account I bear abuse and bother.
Insults surround me, ill reproaches smother.
Even my siblings, children of my mother,
deem me a stranger.

Zeal for your house has totally consumed me.
Those who reproach you censure and abuse me.
When they revile you, they offend and wound me
by their reproaches.

Deaf to my sadness, they abuse my fasting.
Wearing my sackcloth, I can hear them laughing.
Drunkards in public noisily are drafting
ballads about me.

But, as for me, I make a prayer before you,
when it is right, Lord God, again implore you.
Since your salvation ever will endure, you
answer with mercy.

Save me from mud and suffocating mire.
Let me not sink, when everything is dire.
Pluck me from hatred, ever rising higher,
free from the water.

Let not the streaming water overflow me.
Let not the deep rise up to overthrow me.
Do not let Sheol, opening below me,
close and devour me.

Answer my prayer, Lord, in abundant goodness.
Come near to help, with mercy in its fulness.
Hide not your face away, in all my sadness.
Hasten to answer.

Turn to my soul with ransom and redemption.
You know my shame, reproaches and contention,
seeing my hateful foes, in their dissension;
all are before you.

Scorn breaks my heart in sickness and submission,
looking for one to minimise affliction,
one to console and weep for my condition,
but there is no-one.

They gave me poisoned food, when I was yearning,
gave me some vinegar, when I was burning.
Alter to traps their tables, and returning
failure for feasting.

[Ruin their eyes with darkness and delusion.
Weaken their loins with shaking and occlusion.
Let burning anger, frightening confusion,
reach and ensnare them.

Let their encampment be a desolation,
household and tent an empty habitation;
since, on the folk who suffer deprivation,
they have increased pain.

Add to their sins; be ever unforgiving.
Wipe them away from those who are the living,
taking their names from those who are believing.
Show them no mercy.]

When I am poor and driven in vexation,
let saving justice elevate my station,
so I will sing your name with an oblation,
praise and thanksgiving.

This is more pleasing than a gift of oxen;
bulls with their horns and hoofs are all forgotten.
Let those who seek their God, the poor and orphan,
live and be gladdened.

Whenever prayers rise up before the Lord, from
hardship or prison, then the Lord will hear them.
Let praise resound from all in earth and heaven,
everything in them.

God will deliver Zion and her daughters,
building in Judah heritage and quarters;
so may the faithful few, and their supporters,
live there forever.

Psalm 70
DCM
Christmas Carol (Walford Davies)

My God, be pleased to rescue me;
my Lord, give aid today.
Let them be shamed, who all agree
to sweep my soul away.
Let them be driven and debased,
who long for my demise.
Let them return and know disgrace,
who hurl abusive cries.

Let them exult and celebrate,
who seek you and confess.
Let them declare, 'The Lord is great!'
who love your righteousness.
While I am poor and full of strife,
God, answer me today.
You give me help and save my life;
my Lord, do not delay.

Psalm 71
88 88 D
Schmücke Dich

Lord, in you I have been sheltered;
may I never be bewildered.
By your righteousness relieve me;
hear me, save me and receive me.
Be my safe and sturdy stronghold;
be my sure and steady foothold;
be my citadel and refuge;
be my cover from the deluge.

God, release me from the vicious,
from the wicked and malicious.
Lord, my hope and my defender,
from my youth when I was tender,
you, my confidence in trouble,
from my youth in every struggle,
from my mother's womb you brought me,
cut my navel cord, and caught me.

God, in you my praise is constant.
Many see me as a portent.
Lord, you are a mighty shelter,
ever my sufficient helper.
Now my mouth will praise your glory
all the day; do not ignore me,
when in age I am diminished,
when my mortal strength is finished.

Hateful foes who wait to snatch me,
seek my life, and try to catch me,
speak in anger, 'Seize *him*, take *him*,
God has left *him*, none can save *him*.'
Help me now, do not desert me;
may my foes, who seek to hurt me,
face the sound of accusation,
and be wrapped in condemnation.

As I wait with perseverance,
adding praises with persistence,
all day long, with celebration,
telling folk of your salvation,
all your works, in earth and heaven,
number more than I can reckon;
I declare your saving justice,
righteous might, and I proclaim this.

From my youth, when I was tender,
you have guided me; I render
praise to you, for all your wonders,
make you known to many others.
Now, my God, do not forsake me,
though senility may take me,
till I tell your saving strength to
generations, who will praise you.

God, your justice and your power
reach above the highest tower.
Who is like you, when you show me
grief, to try me and to hone me?
All will magnify and praise me,
when you bring me back, to raise me
from the depths of earth, extending
life and comfort, and defending.

I will praise your truth with music,
take my instrument and use it,
melody and praises, ringing
to the Lord, in joy and singing.
Ransomed, I will tell your justice,
how the Lord alone is trusted,
bringing shame upon the rebels,
who have hurt me in my troubles.

Psalm 72
87 87 33 7
Michael

Give the king, my God, your judgement,
virtue to your royal son.
He will judge the people fairly,
and the poor who are undone.
Mountains raise
peace and praise,
for your people, in his days.

He will judge the poor and needy,
crush the ones who bring them low.
He will save the cold and starving,
from oppression and the foe.
He will run,
like the sun,
rising still for years to come.

He will fall like rain in harvest,
making soft both field and fleece.
Righteousness shall bud and blossom,
bringing everlasting peace.
He shall reign,
and obtain
every land and bounding main.

Enemies shall bow before him,
kings of Sheba lick the dust;
kings of Tarshish, and the islands,
bring their tribute and their trust;
princes here
kneel in fear;
all will serve him and revere.

He will save the poor and needy,
help the folk who have no aid.
Freeing them from pain and violence,
he will keep them unafraid,
pity sighs,
hear their cries,
who are precious in his eyes.

He receives his gold from Sheba,
their eternal praise and prayer.
While he lives the land will flourish,
and like Lebanon grow fair.
Tree and tower
thrive and flower,
in his land, through sun and shower.

May his name remain for ever,
live beneath the sun and sky.
May the peoples, by his honour,
bless themselves and magnify,
bless his name,
and acclaim
his position and his fame.

Bless the Lord, the God of Israel,
bless the wonders he has done;
bless his name and mighty splendour,
ever glorious, ever one.
Earth shall then,
once again,
brim with glory. Amen, amen.

Psalm 73
LM
Eisenach

How good to Israel is our God,
to all the folk whose hearts are pure.
But I was nearly overawed,
my faltering steps were insecure.

For I was jealous of the vain,
the boastful, wicked folk at peace.
This side of death they have no pain;
their limbs are flabby and obese.

They do not share in human toil,
they are not smitten like the rest.
Around their neck they wear a coil
of pride; in violence they are dressed.

Their hearts are oozing violent pride;
they pour forth phantasy and crime.
They boast of wealth as they reside,
and plot oppression all the time.

Their mouths are blaring out in heaven,
their tongues go all around the earth.
My people turn to them unbidden;
their days are full, and free from dearth.

They say, 'How can the Most High know?
The Ancient Father has no sense.'
The wicked live secure below,
increasing riches in their tents.

My innocence, it does not pay;
I washed my heart and hands in vain.
For I was stricken all the day,
and censured time and time again.

If I had spoken words like these,
I would have scandalised the just.
I thought it through, and looked for ease,
but I was weary and non-plussed.

I went into your holy space,
and understood their future fate.
Their pathways are a slippery place;
their fall and ruin will be great.

They come to slaughter straight away,
and finished off within a night.
Just like a dream or passing day,
you will despise them in the light.

For I was sour in heart and mind,
oppressed with jealousy and grief.
But I was ignorant and blind,
like brutish beasts in unbelief.

And I am ever with you, Lord;
you hold and keep me by your arm.
You lead and guide me by your word,
and bring me, glorious, safe from harm.

When nothing here on earth will do,
when flesh and heart are overawed,
whom have I now in heaven but you,
my rock, my portion and my God?

For look, the folk who go astray,
as faithless traitors, turn aside,
you judge them so that they decay,
annihilated in their pride.

But as for me, approaching God,
I make the Lord my refuge here.
My life is good beneath your rod,
to tell your works, and make them clear.

Psalm 74

87 87 D
Ebenezer (Ton-Y-Botel)

Why, our God, have you rejected,
poured your wrath upon your sheep?
Call to mind your ransomed people,
see your home in Zion's keep.
Look towards the endless ruins,
all their shouting and disgrace,
foes who stand within your temple,
planting standards in your place.

How they shatter wooden carvings,
like a logger felling trees,
swinging high their blade and hatchet,
smashing doors and sacred frieze!
How they press us altogether,
burning shrines of God around!
They defile your holy temple,
raze your dwelling to the ground.

You have given no more omens,
no more prophet, no more seer,
no-one to foretell the future.
How long shall we live in fear?
how much longer bear reproaches,
their blaspheming, evil curse?
Why do you not reach to save us,
make our brutal foes reverse?

But the God of our salvation
is our ancient King on earth.
You divided up the ocean,
bringing continents to birth;
fed that twisting, primal serpent
to the howling, desert scourge;
splitting spring and mighty torrent,
stemmed the overflowing surge.

Lord, you made the day and evening,
bringing moon and sun to birth,
forming summer heat, and harvest,
fixing boundaries here on earth.
So remember how a senseless
people spurn you, in their war.
Do not let me be devoured,
nor forget your humble poor.

In our darkness, full of violence,
call to mind your covenant here.
Save your needy folk from shame, to
praise you, free from dearth and fear.
Rise, our God; remember curses,
foes blaspheming, plead your case.
Constant imprecations echo;
shame defiles your holy place.

Psalm 75
77 77
Vienna

God, we praise your holy name,
all your wonders, and proclaim,
how your name is ever near;
so we praise you year by year.

I will seize the coming time,
rightly judging acts of crime.
Though the earth and peoples squirm,
I will hold their pillars firm.

You who boast, and vaunt your pride,
wicked, and self-satisfied,
be not boastful, be not proud,
neither let your voice be loud.

Not from east or south or west
is promotion manifest.
God is judge to test and try,
bringing down, and raising high.

From the Lord there is a cup,
mixed and foaming wine to sup;
all the wicked must comply,
drink it down, and drain it dry.

I will sing and ever tell
of the God of Israel.
Slaying wicked to the dust,
God will raise the pure and just.

Psalm 76
66 66 88
Little Cornard

Judah, the home of God,
Jacob, divine ascent,
Salem, the holy sod,
Zion, the sacred tent:
God shattered there the battle bow,
the shield, the sword, and brought them low.

Shining in high renown
over the ancient hills,
ending the wars around,
violence of human wills,
you put the stout of heart to rest;
they fall asleep, and fail the test.

When you rebuke, our God,
rider and horse lie still,
all of them overawed,
empty of aim and will.
Our fearful God of Israel,
when you are angry, none rebel.

Justice in heaven is heard,
fearful, the earth is still,
God as a judge is stirred,
saving the poor at will.
For human rage can only please;
you gird yourself with refugees.

Vow to the Lord your God,
gathering the riches here,
glory in every word,
serving in faith and fear.
For God destroys all human worth,
is feared by every king on earth.

Psalm 77

10 10 10 10 10 10
Song 1

Raising my voice aloud I cry to God,
so he may hear, and listen to my grief.
In my distress, by night I sought you, Lord,
my hand raised up and strong, with no relief.
God, I remember you with my complaint;
I meditate and muse, when I am faint.

You keep my eyelids open, as I sigh;
I am so vexed that words no longer flow.
I ponder long forgotten days gone by,
the ages and the years of long ago.
Remembering joyful music in the night,
with heart and soul I muse and look for light.

Has he, the Lord, rejected us for life?
Will he not show his favour anymore?
Has loving-kindness gone in endless strife?
Is there no future prophecy or law?
The Father of the Years ignores his grace,
encloses love, puts anger in its place.

All my affliction comes from God Most High.
The Lord himself has had a change of heart.
But I remember all the days gone by,
your ancient deeds and actions from the start.
I meditate on all your works and ways;
I contemplate your acts of former days.

God, in the sanctuary where your face appears,
is there a Father who compares with you?
Yours are the wonders, Father of the Years;
yours is the strength for everyone to view,
redeeming Jacob by your mighty arm,
the tribe of Joseph, freeing them from harm.

Primeval waters saw you, mighty God,
the waters saw and writhed in anguished birth;
the very deeps in fear were overawed,
your clouds poured out their deluge on the earth.
Your thunder clouds were crashing overhead;
your flashing arrows filled the world with dread.

Thunder and whirlwind rumbled in the sky,
with lightning flashes blazing by decree;
the earth was trembling, as you passed near by,
with hidden steps, your pathway in the sea.
You led your people like a flock of sheep,
by Moses and by Aaron, through the deep.

Psalm 78
DCM
Kingsfold, First Mode Melody, Third Mode Melody

Give ear, my people, to my law;
hear what I have to say,
as I interpret mysteries here,
from ancient times today.
What we have heard we now record
for children yet unborn,
the strength and wonders of the Lord,
to praise him, and to warn.

In Jacob, God has set his charge,
his law in Israel,
commanding us to make it known
to unborn folk as well,
so they in turn might pass it on
to their own children too,
that they might put their trust in God,
in everything they do.

Then they should not forget their God,
but guard his ancient laws,
and not be like their forebears, who
refused them, every clause,
a stubborn and rebellious breed,
of fickle heart and mind,
unfaithful to the God of Years,
their spirits disinclined.

The archers out of Ephraim
turned back when there was war.
They did not keep his covenant firm,
but sinned when they forswore,
refused to walk within God's law,
forgot his mighty deeds,
the wonders, which he showed to them,
before the Sea of Reeds.

He showed their parents wonders, down
in Egypt, Zoan's field.
He split the sea, and led them through;
the waters were congealed.
He led them with a cloud by day,
and fire to shine at night.
He split the rocks across the waste,
brought gushing springs to light.

He gave them streams from rocky crags;
the rivers ran and flowed.
But they increased their treason there,
against their Most High God.
Those rebels turned and tested him,
demanding food as well.
They insolently asked for more,
a blasphemous cartel.

'Can God, the Father of the Years,
give flesh for us to eat?
He may have made the rock produce
a flood in all this heat,
he may have made the waterfall
remarkably appear,
but can he also give us bread,
or lay a table here?'

The Lord was angry when he heard;
in Jacob there was fire.
Yes, wrath went up in Israel
from God, his burning ire.
For they did not believe in him,
or trust his saving hand.
They put no faith in God, but still
he issued his command.

He summoned all the clouds above,
and opened up the sky,
unlocked the doors of heaven to rain
his manna from on high;
he gave on earth the food of heaven,
until they were replete,
the table of the sons of God,
for humankind to eat.

He called a tempest from the east,
he drove it from the south,
he rained upon them flesh as dust,
to fill up every mouth.
The birds fell round about their tents,
as thick as piles of sand;
they gorged themselves, and their desire
was met by his command.

Yet while they were still eating there,
the food still in their throat,
the wrath of God came up on them,
and slew the men of note,
laid low the youth of Israel,
but still they went astray.
For disbelief he snuffed them out,
in terror and dismay.

When God had struck them down they turned
and sought his face with tears,
remembering he was still their rock,
the Father of the Years,
how God Most High redeemed them, when
they cried to him for aid,
but they were only lying words,
a cynical parade.

They did not keep his covenant firm;
they were not true within.
But his compassion still was great,
forgiving all their sin.
He turned his anger far away,
yes, time and time again;
he did not ruin them in full,
or let his wrath remain.

He kept in mind that they were flesh,
a wind that disappears.
How often they rebelled and grieved
the Father of the Years.
They turned and put him to the test,
in howling desert waste.
The Holy One of Israel,
was filled with bitter haste.

They did not call to mind the day
his hand had brought them out,
from Egypt, and from Zoan's field,
with wonders round about.
He turned their waters into blood,
which they could never drink.
He sent his swarms to eat them up,
and frogs to make them stink.

He brought a plague of locusts, to
devour their harvest yield,
he blasted vines and fruitful trees,
with hail in every field,
delivering cattle to their deaths,
by lightning bolt and fire.
He sent his messengers of doom,
his anger, wrath and ire.

He made a highway for his wrath,
to drive their souls to death,
delivering them to deadly plague,
to take away their breath.
He struck their firstborn in the land,
in Egypt, every one.
The tents of Ham each loved and lost
their first and eldest son.

He pulled his people out like sheep,
and drove them like a herd,
through trackless sand and desert waste,
to safety by his word.
They did not fear their hateful foes,
who drowned beneath the sea.
He brought them to his holy land
and hill, by his decree.

He drove the nations out before
the tribes of Israel,
allotted them their holy land,
to pitch their tents and dwell.
Like broken bows they tested God
Most High, and turned away.
Just as their forebears they rebelled,
were swift to disobey.

They vexed him with their empty gods,
on hill and mountain height.
God heard, and in his jealous wrath,
rejected Jacob's might.
Forsaking Shiloh's holy place
to hateful foe and flames,
he gave their strength and beauty to
captivity and chains.

He gave his people to the sword,
was wroth with his estate.
Their young men fell to fire and flame,
their maidens to their fate;
their priests were slaughtered by the sword,
their widows did not weep.
But, like a hero after wine,
the Lord awoke from sleep.

He struck his hateful foes behind,
destroyed their great esteem,
rejected Joseph and his tent,
the tribe of Ephraim.
He chose the tribe of Judah, and
Mount Zion, which he loved.
He built his temple as the heights,
established and approved.

He chose his servant David, when
he took him from the sheep;
from nursing ewes he brought him near,
put Jacob in his keep.
He ruled in Jacob as their king,
to pasture and to spare;
he guided them with skilful hand,
and single-minded care.

Psalm 79
CM
Bangor, Burford

O God, the nations have defiled
your temple in their lust,
attacked your heritage, and razed
Jerusalem to dust.

They gave the bodies of our dead,
as food for birds to eat,
the flesh of all your faithful ones
to beasts and birds as meat.

They poured our blood upon the earth,
like water all around,
and in Jerusalem is none
to place them in the ground.

So we became a laughing-stock
in every neighbour state,
the scorn and ridicule of those
around, who denigrate.

How long, O Lord, will you be full
of jealousy and fire,
will you continue pouring forth
your burning wrath and ire?

Pour out your wrath on people, who
have never known you, Lord,
the kingdoms, who have never called
upon your name or word.

For they have wasted Jacob, and
devoured him everywhere,
they devastated house and home
and habitation there.

Do not remember former sins,
for we are very low,
but let your mercy quickly come
to meet us here below.

So help us now, O saving God,
and call to mind your name;
forgive our guilty hearts, protect
the glory of your fame.

Why should the nations say of you,
'Where is their God and aid?'
Let vengeance for your servants' blood
be openly displayed.

Let groaning sighs of prisoners here
rise up before your eye,
and let your mighty arm redeem
the folk condemned to die.

Turn back upon our neighbour states
their blasphemy and bane,
reward them seven times as much,
who ridicule your name.

So we your people, we your sheep,
will praise you evermore,
and tell your praise for years to come,
acclaim you and adore.

Psalm 80
898 898 664 88
Wachet Auf

Israel's Shepherd, pay attention,
and, guarding Joseph from aggression,
rise up for us to take your stand.
From your cherubim attendants,
shine forth on us, his poor descendants,
and save us by your mighty hand -
Manasseh, Benjamin,
the tribe of Ephraim -
God of Israel.
Shine from your place and show your face,
to bring us back with saving grace.

God of armies, how much longer?
How long will wrath and smoking anger
remain your answer to our prayer?
Lord, you give us bread for sighing,
with tears to drink, forever crying.
You do not seem to see or care.
The scoffing and disdain
of friend and foe remain,
God of armies.
Shine from your place and show your face,
to bring us back with saving grace.

Out of Egypt you transplanted
a vine, to fields that you had granted,
removing nations by your hand.
As you cleared the soil around it,
its roots dug down to feed and ground it,
until it stretched across the land.
It covered every sod,
was like the trees of God
on the mountains,
its branches free to reach the sea,
and to the river, by decree.

Why have you destroyed its hedges,
so passers-by encroach the edges?
They pluck its fruit to take away.
Forest animals uproot it,
and unclean insects quite pollute it;
O God of Hosts, turn back, we pray.
Look down from heaven and see
this vine of your decree,
and protect it.
Guard and refine your stock, your vine;
protect with might our royal line.

See how we are burned with fire,
cut off by every occupier.
Destroy them by your strong reproach.
May your hand be on your servant,
to make him strong and truly fervent,
so we may constantly approach.
Revive us in our shame,
to call upon your name,
Lord of armies.
Shine from your place and show your face,
to bring us back with saving grace.

Psalm 81

LM
Agincourt (Deo Gratias)

Rejoice and shout to God our might,
the God of Jacob, our delight,
and raise a song with harp and lyre,
to cymbal and melodious choir.

With trumpet blast we must appear,
in holy convocation here,
at new and full moon by decree,
for sacred feast and jubilee.

This law was laid in Israel,
a rule for Joseph to retell,
when Jacob's God had set him free
from Egypt's rule and slavery.

I heard a voice I did not know.
'I freed you from your toil below,
removed the burden from your back,
the picks and bricks and heavy pack.

'You cried when they molested you;
in Meribah I tested you,
and from my dark and stormy place,
I answered when you saw my face.

'Give ear, my people Israel,
that I may testify and tell,
how seldom I became your choice;
if only you would hear my voice!

'You shall not keep a foreign god,
or worship idols, overawed,
for I, the Lord, am God, who brought
you up from Egypt to my court.

'But Israel would not obey,
rejecting me, they went astray.
I drove them far with stubborn breast,
to wander off at their behest.

'If only Israel would hear,
to follow me in faith and fear.
I would have made their enemies
lamentable nonentities.

'I would have brought my hand around,
to cast their foes upon the ground.
So those who hated me would meet,
to cringe before me at my feet.

'Then I would feed them with my stock,
of wheat and honey from the rock.
So open wide your mouth, and I
will feed you from my store on high.'

Psalm 82
76 76 D
King's Lynn

God stands in his assembly
of heaven, to judge the gods.
'How long will you be friendly
to vile and evil squads?
Give justice to the orphan,
the righteous and the poor,
restore them from misfortune,
from harsh abuse and war.

'Deliver all the needy
from wickedness and wrong.
Restrain and stop the greedy,
the evil, and the strong.
They have no understanding,
no sense of what is right.
With wickedness expanding,
they wander in the night.

'The powers that be are failing;
the earth is out of course.
Though you have been prevailing,
as gods in heaven's high court,
from now you are redundant,
from now on you will die.'
Rise up, our God, for judgement,
possess the earth on high.

Psalm 83
87 87 D
Ebenezer (Ton-Y-Botel)

[God, do not remain so quiet,
be not silent, be not still.
Look, your hateful foes are roaring,
those who hate you march and drill.
They are plotting crafty counsel,
watching folk that you hold dear:
'Let us wipe them out, and finish
Israel as a nation here.'

They consult with one objective,
make a deal to come and fight.
Hagar, Moab plan together,
Edom and the Ishmaelite.
Gebal, Amon, Amalek, with
Philistines and those of Tyre,
while Assyria also moves, to
help the heirs of Lot, for hire.

Make them into dung like Midian,
Sisera and Jabin too,
butchered at the Wadi Kishon,
slain at Endor, in our view,
just as Zebah and Zalmunnah
who, with Oreb and with Zeeb,
planned to take to their possession
sacred field and holy glebe.

Make them like a stormy tempest,
chaff and dust before the wind,
burning like a forest fire,
leaving only ash behind.
Make them like a flame, that sets the
mountains and the hills alight.
This is how you will pursue them,
terrified and put to flight.

Let them know humiliation,
scorn, dishonour and disgrace,
so that they may seek your favour,
Lord, your favour and your face.
Let them all be shamed and daunted,
let them fall and pass away,
knowing, that in all creation,
you, the Lord Most High, hold sway.]

Psalm 84
78 78 88
Liebster Jesu

Lord, how lovely are your courts,
in your holy habitation.
All my longing, all my thoughts,
focus on your royal station.
Heart and flesh ring out their glory
to the Father of their story.

Here the swallow makes her nest,
here the birds have your protection.
Lord of Hosts, they hatch and rest,
near your altar and affection.
Blessed are those who ever dwell here,
praising you, and serve you well here.

Blessed are those with you for strength,
walking highways of affliction,
through the valleys, where, at length,
rain will clothe with benediction.
Strong and stronger, they rely on
God, to bring them home to Zion.

Lord of Hosts, receive my prayer,
God and King, grant my petition.
God of Jacob, turn your ear
to my passionate submission.
Look upon our shield appointed,
see the face of your anointed.

I am longing to adore,
just one day, within your temple,
better than a thousand more,
where the evil folk assemble.
I would rather guard your threshold,
than inhabit wicked households.

God, the Lord, is sun and shield,
giving grace and glory freely,
never keeping goodness sealed
from the just, who walk discreetly.
Lord of Hosts, though we are dust, you
bless the folk, who ever trust you.

Psalm 85
87 87 D
Hyfrydol, Corvedale

You, O Lord, were pleased to save your
land and folk, when they were slaves,
bearing Jacob's violation,
clearing all our sinful graves.
You have gathered up your fury,
turned away your blazing wrath,
brought your people back from bondage,
safely on their homeward path.

Turn us, God of our salvation,
let your anger pass away.
Will there always be vexation,
will your anger ever stay?
Will you not revive your people,
so they may rejoice again?
Show your grace and loving-kindness,
save your people from their pain.

Now the Father of the Years will
speak, and I will listen well.
Now the Lord will speak of peace, for
all his people Israel,
peace for all the faithful, lest they
turn to folly, underhand.
Your salvation rests upon us;
glory shines across our land.

Grace and truth have met together,
peace and justice kiss in love.
Truth shall spring from earth, with justice
gazing down from heaven above.
Yes, the Lord will pour his blessing
on the land, to make it grow.
Justice will go forth before him,
lay the path of God below.

Psalm 86
76 76 D
King's Lynn

Hear me, O Lord, and answer
my poverty and need.
Protect me from disaster,
O save me and give heed.
I am your faithful servant,
I put my trust in you.
Be gracious and observant;
I call the whole day through.

Give ear to my petition,
and listen to my prayer.
I call in desperation,
for you will surely care.
Give joy to me, your servant;
I raise my weary soul.
Lord, you are good and fervent,
forgiving all who call.

No other god is like you,
O Lord, the God of all,
for you have given life to
the nations, great and small.
They worship their defender,
and glorify your name,
for you, their might and splendour,
alone remain the same.

O Lord, make known your pathways,
and I will follow you.
Lord, may my spirit always
be honourable and true,
my Lord and God, to fear you,
to glorify and praise.
In mercy bring me near you,
from Sheol's deadly shades.

The insolent have risen,
they cruelly seek my soul.
O God, they have no vision
of godliness at all.
But you, my Lord and Father
of Years, are God above,
compassionate, the author
of gracious truth and love.

So turn and show your mercy,
to strengthen and secure;
although I am unworthy,
deliver and restore;
come, show some gracious token,
which those who hate may see,
that you, my Lord, have spoken;
give aid to set me free.

Psalm 87

66 11 66 11
Down Ampney

Founded on holy heights,
in her the Lord delights,
loves Zion more than Jacob's habitations,
splendid in gate and wall,
honoured above them all,
the city of our God for generations.

Babylon comes to mind,
Rahab and all its kind,
while I remember all of those who know me.
Even the Philistines,
Tyre where the ocean shines,
and Cush - they all were born in her below me.

Zion they all prefer;
it will be said of her,
'Now everyone on earth is born within you.'
God, the Most High, is here,
builder and overseer,
establishing your palaces to win you.

And when the nations come,
peoples beneath the sun,
our Lord will count their number on her mountains.
All will be gathered here,
born equal, to appear,
with song and dance, as living springs and fountains.

Psalm 88
76 76 D
Passion Chorale

Lord God of my salvation,
by day and night I call.
Receive my keen oblation,
give ear to sigh and gall.
My soul is full of evil,
in Sheol, in the pit,
where there is no retrieval,
and no-one will acquit.

I lie with the departed,
adrift among the dead,
with corpses, disregarded
by you, and lost in dread.
Cut off from your protection,
in deepest hell below,
you place me in subjection,
in death and overthrow.

Your anger weighs upon me,
afflicted by your waves.
You place me, lost and lonely,
forlorn among the graves.
You make my life offensive,
you drive my friends away,
enclosed and apprehensive,
with no-one who will stay.

Because of my affliction
my vision fades away.
O Lord, in dereliction
I yearn through all the day.
Is there a sign or wonder,
your tokens for the dead?
Will shades arise to honour,
in piety and dread?

And will your loving-kindness
be told among the graves?
your faithfulness, where blindness
encloses and enslaves?
your justice in destruction?
your wonders in the dark?
your knowledge and instruction,
where spirits disembark?

I call you to restore me;
at daybreak hear my prayer.
So why do you ignore me,
and hide away your care?
O Lord, I have been dying,
and needy from my youth,
my soul in terror crying,
bewildered by your truth.

Your anger passes through me,
your terrors bring me down.
They circle and pursue me,
they inundate and drown.
You take away my dearest;
they leave me to descend,
to where the dark is nearest,
my one and only friend.

Psalm 89, Part 1
DCM
Christmas Carol (Walford Davies)

My Lord, I sing forever of
your love and faithful care,
for all the children yet to come,
affirm it and declare.
From age to age, and year to year,
just as the heavens above,
your faithful care, forever firm,
is everlasting love.

'I made a lasting covenant here,
with David my elect.
I now affirm your seed, your throne,
established and select.'
The heavens adore your wonders, Lord,
among the gods above.
For who in heaven is like the Lord,
for faithful care and love?

The Father of the gods is feared
by courtiers, who surround,
the Lord of Hosts, their mighty God,
with faithful mercy crowned.
You rule the sea in splendid power,
you still its stormy main,
and, crushing Rahab as the dead,
your foes with mighty reign.

The heavens are yours, the earth as well,
the world, and all its store.
You laid them out, and they are firm,
established evermore,
creating all, both north and south,
to praise you and acclaim;
Mount Tabor and Mount Hermon sing,
to glorify your name.

Your hand is strong, with power and might,
your right hand will ascend.
Your throne is built on righteousness,
while love and truth attend.
Blessed are the people who will stand,
to worship and acclaim.
They walk before you, Lord, in light,
rejoicing in your name.

Your righteousness will raise them up,
exalt their pride and power.
You are the beauty, mighty strength;
your favour is a tower.
Our king, our shield, belongs to God,
the holy one, the Lord,
in Israel, since days of old,
when prophets spoke this word.

'I placed a crown upon the head
of David, my elect,
my servant and my chosen one,
to govern and direct.
My holy oil, upon his head,
has made his line secure;
made firm by me, my mighty hand
and strength will make him sure.

'No hateful foes will lend to him,
no traitor bring him low,
for I will drive attackers down,
for him defeat the foe.
My faithful care and love will be
forever there beside;
his horn will be exalted in
my name, and glorified.

'Yes, he will reign across the sea,
and through the river lands,
declare of me, "Eternal rock,
my Father, who commands,
my saviour and my ancient God!"
Indeed, beneath the sun,
to other kings he is most high,
my first and only son.

'My love for him I keep secure
beside me, as before.
This covenant I now make with him
will stand for evermore.
His seed will last from year to year,
and, never to decline,
his throne to me, as heaven above,
an everlasting sign.

'Though children of his line forsake
me, wander from my laws,
profaning me, or my decrees,
my statutes, any clause,
though I may beat them for their sin,
and visit my redress,
no, never will my faith depart,
or break in faithlessness.

'My covenant here will never change,
my word will never break.
To David I will never lie,
and I will not forsake.
His seed will last for evermore,
his throne be like the sun,
established as the moon above,
a sign to run and run.'

Psalm 89, Part 2
DCM
Third Mode Melody

But you have spurned and cast away,
you rouse yourself to wrath.
You change your covenant, break your word,
reverse your servant's path.
You pour dishonour on his crown,
you bring him to the ground.
You ruin every citadel;
you break his walls around.

And passers-by, they lay him waste,
our neighbours curse his name,
his hateful foes are lifted up,
rejoicing in his shame.
Yes, you have turned his sword away,
subdued him in the fight,
you cast his throne across the earth,
extinguishing his light.

Diminishing his youthful days,
and clothing him in shame,
how long will you remain concealed,
how long will anger flame?
Remember me, my mortal lot,
my fleeting human life.
What point is there in living on,
when all we see is strife?

Lord, where are those who never die,
who live for evermore?
Can one deliver us from death,
avoiding Sheol's door?
Remember, Lord, the brazen curse,
the peoples who encroach,
and how your servants bear within
your foes, and their reproach.

Where are your faithful care and love,
the covenant that you swore?
Are David and his royal line
important anymore?
Your royal crown, your chosen son,
is slighted once again,
but blessed on high be God the Lord
for ever, and amen.

Psalm 90
87 87 87
Pange Lingua

Lord, you are our home and dwelling,
through the ages of the earth.
Well before the hills were forming,
writhing in the pains of birth,
from forever to forever
you are God, who called them forth.

Father of the Years, you made us,
and with dust we reunite:
'Go back down, you mortal children,
back to darkness, out of sight.'
For to you a thousand years are
as a day, or passing night.

As a dream they pass before you,
overwhelmed and fast asleep;
in the morning, like the grassland,
fresh and flourishing and deep;
In the evening, dry and withered,
as the passing ages sweep.

We are ended in your anger,
dreading terror from on high.
You have set our sins before you;
secrets lie before your eye.
All our days dissolve in fury,
and our years are as a sigh.

Human lives are seven decades,
eight for those with strength to stay;
they are only full of trouble,
full of sorrow and decay.
All our days and years are failing,
speeding as we fly away.

Who can know your mighty anger,
who can know your fury here?
Those, who honour and revere you,
know your fury in their fear.
May we count our days in wisdom,
knowing we will disappear.

Lord, return towards your servants;
how much more will you delay?
Fill us with your loving-kindness,
in the morning, with the day.
So may we rejoice before you,
ever singing as we pray.

Gladden us for all the trouble,
days of toil and years of pain.
Show your servants, God, the splendour
of your work, and loving reign.
Lord, establish our endeavour,
prosper all our work again.

Psalm 91

88 88 88
Melita

The one who dwells beneath the shade
of God Almighty, unafraid,
will say to God in all events,
'The Lord Most High is my defence.
Whatever evil may pursue,
my refuge, I will trust in you.'

For God will save you from the snare,
from yawning chasm or despair.
Though pestilence or curse pursue,
your God will calm and cover you.
Beneath his wings and holy down,
his truth will shield you all around.

Be not afraid of mighty dread,
or flying arrow overhead,
of terror lurking in the dark,
of battle or the evil mark,
of stalking pestilence by night,
or deadly sickness in the light.

Though thousands and ten thousands die,
and death extinguishes the eye,
though many perish, ills appear,
no plague will touch you or come near.
Yes, you will see the wicked fall,
and retribution on them all.

You made the Lord and God Most High
your shelter from the battle cry,
so lurking evil or dissent
will not come near or plague your tent.
Your God commands an angel host,
to guard you from their heavenly post.

They bear you safely in their hand,
preserve your life at my command,
in case you fall and break a bone,
or strike your foot against a stone.
You trample every lion down,
and grind the snake into the ground.

Because in love you cling to me,
and know my name, I set you free.
Whatever trouble may pursue,
I answer now, and honour you.
Your soul will overflow to praise
in freedom, for eternal days.

Psalm 92
LM
Song 34

How good to praise the Lord above,
to sing your name with great delight,
Most High, with dawn, declare your love,
praising your truth at dead of night.

Playing upon the harp and strings,
with lute and song before the Lord.
All of your deeds my being sings,
ringing my joy with every chord.

How great are all your deeds, O Lord;
your thoughts and plans are very deep.
Fools cannot understand your word,
or ever know how you will reap.

Though wicked people grow as grass,
and evildoers thrive and flower,
they are destroyed as ages pass;
you, though, O Lord, are raised in power.

All of your hateful foes, O Lord,
your hateful foes will die away,
those who work evil are outpoured,
scattered around in disarray.

I am exalted like an ox,
and richly blessed with holy oil,
hearing the doom of those who watch,
seeing my boasting foes recoil.

Those who are righteous grow, as palms
in Lebanon, before the Lord,
cedars replanted here with psalms,
into the courts and house of God.

Here they will bloom and richly grow,
still bearing fruit in agéd stock.
Here they declare to all below,
justice is from the Lord, my rock.

Psalm 93
664 6664
Moscow

Worship the Lord, the King,
high over everything.
Worship the King,
girded in majesty,
strength and nobility,
vested with dignity.
Worship the King.

Wonders on earth unknown
form your eternal throne;
you are our King.
Torrent and river flow,
rising to overthrow,
rising from long ago.
You, Lord, are King.

Thundering, mighty sea,
pounding in majesty,
river and spring -
you keep them all away,
binding them every day,
higher in every way.
You, Lord, are King.

You, Lord, are King for sure,
righteous in rule and law,
so we will sing:
temple of loveliness,
endless in holiness.
Ceaselessly we confess,
you, Lord, are King.

Psalm 94

10 10 10 10 10 10
Unde et Memores

O God of vengeance, Father of the Years,
O God of anger, shine upon the earth.
Be lifted up, O Lord, to judge our tears,
bring back upon the proud as they deserve.
How long, O Lord, shall wicked folk insult?
How long, O Lord, shall wickedness exult?

The evil doers boast, they pour conceit,
they crush your heritage, the folk you own.
They murder, Lord, the stranger in the street,
the widow and the orphan, as they groan.
They say, 'The God of Jacob does not care.'
They say of you, 'The Lord is unaware.'

But he who made the ear can surely hear.
The one who formed the eye cannot be blind.
The Lord who judges nations will appear,
to discipline, rebuking humankind.
You heartless, brutish fools, consider this.
How long will you so stupidly dismiss?

The Lord perceives the thoughts of humankind,
that we are mortal, only passing breath.
Blessed are the folk you teach, to keep confined
within your laws, preserved and free from death,
serene and peaceful, safe in days of pain,
while pits will snare as one the inhumane.

O Lord, you will not leave the people here,
abandon or forsake the folk you own,
for justice will return to those who fear,
from age to age, in truth and mercy known,
while those of upright heart shall surely know,
and follow after justice as they go.

So who is there to stand, be by my side,
against the evildoers and the base?
If he, the Lord, were not a help or guide,
my soul would soon be silenced in disgrace.
But when I said, 'My foot will surely slide,'
your mercy, Lord, supported me inside.

When hordes of restless thoughts assault my bones,
your solace comes to calm and comfort me.
Will you be joined with devastating thrones,
who implement injustice by decree?
They persecute and victimise the just,
condemning guiltless blood for wicked lust.

The Lord will be protection from attack,
and God is my defence and sturdy rock.
My God will turn their wickednesses back,
on those who are a base and sinful stock.
The Lord our God will slay them for their crime,
the Lord will surely slay them in their prime.

Psalm 95
10 11 11 12
Slane

Come, let us ring out our joy to the Lord,
with cheering, thanksgiving and shouting to God,
our rock and salvation to whom we resort,
our King and great Father of the heavenly court.

God's is the power that fashioned the earth,
and brought all the peaks of the mountains to birth,
who made the wide oceans and all they contain,
establishing dry land and the natural domain.

Come, let us honour, bow down and revere
the Lord, who has made us, and kneel down in fear,
for we are his sheep in the pasture of God,
protected and guided by a merciful rod.

[O that today you would listen to me!
Do not close your heart as they did by the sea.
Your forebears at Massah, and Meribah's well,
ignoring my wonders, fell away and rebelled.

Forty years long I despised them and said,
'This people are erring in heart and in head,
not knowing my ways,' so in anger I stressed,
'These rebels will never ever enter my rest.']

Psalm 96
10 10 11 11
Laudate Dominum (Parry)

Sing out to the Lord,
bring new songs to birth.
Sing out to the Lord,
all creatures on earth,
Sing out, every nation,
and daily proclaim
the Lord's great salvation,
his wonderful name.

For great is the Lord,
and worthy of praise,
above every god,
revered in his ways.
Declare, every nation,
his glorious name,
in every location,
his wonderful fame.

The gods of the world
are worthless and vain.
The Lord has unfurled
his heavenly reign,
creating the splendour
of temple and sky,
our mighty defender,
in beauty on high.

Acknowledge the Lord,
all peoples on earth,
acknowledge the Lord,
his glorious worth.
Acknowledge his splendour,
the name of the Lord.
Bring presents to enter
the temple of God.

Bow down to the Lord
all over the earth,
with holy accord
acknowledge his worth.
With great celebration
let everyone sing,
proclaim to the nations,
'The Lord, he is King!'

Let heaven proclaim,
creation rejoice;
let oceans acclaim,
with thundering voice.
Let everything living
exult in the field;
let trees, with thanksgiving,
ring out from the weald.

The world is secure
and never to fall;
the Lord will ensure
true judgement for all,
who comes with his sentence,
who comes with his grace,
with righteous ascendance,
through all time and space.

Psalm 97
87 87 D
Austria

God the Lord is King for ever -
let the isles and earth rejoice,
cloudy darkness for a cover -
sing together with one voice:
righteousness, eternal justice,
firm supports beneath the throne,
blazing fire before and after,
his defeated foes will groan.

Lightning flashes through creation,
melting ancient hills in fear,
shaking earth to its foundation,
as the Lord of all draws near.
Heaven tells his righteous story -
praise the Lord of all the earth.
Every people sees the glory,
all as one proclaim his worth.

All who worship molten fetish,
worthless gods of human hands,
they will be ashamed and perish,
when the Lord Most High commands.
May their gods bow down to praise you.
Zion heard; may Judah sing,
sing your justice, Lord, to raise you
far above their gods, as King.

Lord, you hate the evildoer,
keeping all whose souls are just,
freeing them from wicked power,
as they offer you their trust.
Light is sown for all the righteous,
joy for every noble face.
Praise the Lord, rejoice, you righteous,
for a token of his grace.

Psalm 98
87 87 D
Abbot's Leigh

Sing afresh in all creation,
sing the wonders of the Lord.
He has shown his great salvation,
bared his holy arm abroad.
He revealed his righteous favour,
everywhere the nations dwell,
called to mind his truth, the saviour
of the house of Israel.

Earth's remotest bounds have noted
God's salvation, and his worth.
Shout aloud with songs, devoted
to the Lord of all the earth.
With the lyre, the lyre and dancing,
play before the Lord, and sing.
With a trumpet fanfare blasting,
shout before the Lord, the King.

Let the sea in fullness thunder,
all that lives across the earth.
Rivers, clap your hands in wonder,
mountains, cry aloud with mirth.
For the Lord, in full ascendance,
comes with righteousness unfurled.
He will judge, with upright sentence,
all the peoples of the world.

Psalm 99
14 14 4 7 8
Lobe Den Herren

Our Lord is King, so may peoples with trembling implore
him.
Seated on cherubim, let earth below quake before him.
Fearful in fame,
highly exalted in name,
holy in Zion - adore him.

Strength of the king, who loves fairness and right for the
lowly,
justice in Jacob is founded by you, and you only.
Worship our God,
bow to his footstool and rod.
He, the Lord God, he is holy.

Moses and Aaron, with priests of the Lord, who ordained them,
Samuel, with those who appealed, and he quickly sustained them -
God answered loud,
spoke from the pillar of cloud -
they kept his laws and explained them.

You, Lord our God, alone, pardoned and answered them duly,
Father of Years, but with vengeance, when they were unruly.
Worship our God,
high on his mountain and sod.
He, the Lord God, he is holy.

Psalm 100
888 with Alleluia
Victory, Gelobt sei Gott

[Alleluia, alleluia, alleluia.]
Shout to the Lord in every place,
worship with joy in every race,
sing to the Lord before his face.
Alleluia.

Know that the Lord alone is God;
we are the people of the Lord,
sheep of his flock beneath his rod.
Alleluia.

Enter his gates with songs to raise,
enter his courts with thanks and praise,
bless him forever, all his ways.
Alleluia.

For he is good, the Lord is sure;
mercy and truth from him endure,
steadfast and firm for evermore.
Alleluia.
[Alleluia, alleluia, alleluia.]

Psalm 101
74 74 D
Gwalchmai

Love and justice I will sing,
Lord, before you,
pleasing music I will bring
to adore you.
I will be completely sound,
- when will you come? -
and in virtue, I will ground
my entire home.

Worthless matters in my sight,
I reject them.
Traitors, who are brought to light,
I eject them.
Twisted hearts I turn aside
from my presence.
Wicked folk will not abide
in attendance.

Those who slander, those who spy,
I will slay them.
Boastful heart and haughty eye,
I shall weigh them.
I will look for honest friends
to preserve me.
Those of sound and noble ends,
they shall serve me.

[Evil traitors in the land,
every liar,
with the wicked, will be banned
from my hire.
Every morning by the sword
I will slay them,
from the city of the Lord,
end their mayhem.]

Psalm 102
88 88 6
St. Margaret

Good Lord, receive my humble prayer,
and pay attention to my plea.
Hide not your face or loving care,
and, when distress and grief ensnare,
come quickly, answer me.

My days are finished in the smoke;
my bones are burning up inside.
My bread is bitter, and I choke;
my heart, beneath your heavy stroke,
is withered up and dried.

I groan and murmur all the day;
my bones are clinging to my skin.
I live alone, and far away,
an owl in ruin and decay,
a wilderness within.

Awake, I flutter to and fro,
some lonely bird upon a roof.
All day my enemies, I know,
are using me to curse, and, oh,
I must endure reproof.

My food is ashes for my bread.
My drink is mingling with my grief.
Your wrath has burst upon my head;
you toss me out, as something dead,
and I have no relief.

My days go down into the shade;
my life is dying as the grass.
But you, my Lord, are unafraid;
your name will never, ever fade,
as mortal ages pass.

You rise to pity and to hear,
for Zion's ruin is unjust,
and now the time of grace is near;
to us, your servants, she is dear,
her very stones and dust.

Then all the nations will revere;
their kings will glorify your name,
when in your glory you appear,
to build in Zion, and to clear,
to save our souls from shame.

The Lord will look upon our prayer,
our destitution, and the sword;
we now record it, and declare,
so every family, and heir,
may rise to praise the Lord.

The Lord examined in his place,
surveying all the earth on high,
to hear the groaning in the gates,
our prisoners lying in disgrace,
and all condemned to die.

When peoples gather to acclaim,
in Zion, to adore the Lord,
humanity will serve your name,
and, in Jerusalem, proclaim,
that you alone are God.

My God afflicted all my ways;
my passing, mortal life is frail.
I said, 'Do not reduce my days,
eternal Father of my praise;
for you will never fail.'

In former days you made the earth,
established heaven by your hand;
while they will perish in their dearth,
as clothes or rags of little worth,
you will forever stand.

You change them, they will not endure,
but you, your years will never cease.
Your servants' children will be sure;
their seed will ever live secure,
to serve their God in peace.

Psalm 103
87 87 87
Regent Square

Bless the Lord, my soul, within me,
all I am, his holy name.
Bless the Lord, my soul, and in me
ever call to mind his fame,
who forgives your sin and error,
healing every ill and shame.

He redeems you from the grave, to
crown your life with love and care,
satisfies with life, to save you,
as an eagle in the air.
He, the Lord, in righteous judgement,
acts for those in deep despair.

He has shown himself to Moses,
all his deeds to Israel.
He, the Lord, is kind, and shows his
grace and love, when we rebel.
He is patient, slow to anger;
burning fury will dispel.

He does not rebound upon us
consequences for our shame.
He does not bear down upon us
our iniquity and blame,
high as heaven his loving-kindness,
poured on those who fear his name.

He, the Lord, removes offences,
as the east is from the west.
As a father's loving sense is,
so his love burns in his breast.
He remembers we are dust; he
knows we are a passing guest.

Human souls are like the grasses,
flowering fresh, in stalk and ear:
when the wind is strong, and passes,
we decay and disappear;
but the Lord remains forever,
showing love for those who fear.

He will make his victory clear, to
children's children, as before,
founding truth when they revere, who
keep his covenant and his law.
High in heaven he set his throne, as
Lord of all for evermore.

Bless the Lord, angelic courses,
mighty ones, who do his word.
Bless the Lord, obedient forces,
all who serve his great reward.
May the whole created order
join, to praise and bless the Lord.

Psalm 104
13 13 13 13 13 13
Thaxted

My soul, now bless the Lord, my
great God and Lord of might!
Adorned in veneration,
you wrap yourself in light.
You stretch the tent of heaven,
you set your chambers fast,
their beams above the waters,
to hold them, and to last.
You make the cloud a chariot,
to fly across the sky,
your angels blazing onwards,
as wind and fire on high.

You founded earth forever,
established and secure,
when deeps were overwhelming
the mountain heights before.
At your rebuke the waters
subsided in alarm,
from hill to valley fleeing,
to where they do no harm,
the places you appointed,
to hold them and restrain,
so never more returning
to flood the earth again.

You pour the springs, emerging
through rill and mountain lea,
to quench the thirsty cattle,
and asses running free.
The birds of heaven nesting,
in branches where they sing,
you shower from your chambers,
to water land and spring,
and, far from any fountain,
where ibises reside,
the high and craggy mountain,
with coney nests inside.

You make the grass for cattle,
and herb for humankind,
you give us wine for drinking,
to gladden heart and mind,
producing food to nourish,
from deep within the soil,
to make the heart emboldened,
and faces shine with oil.
You sow the trees of God, and
they grow at your request,
in Lebanon, the cedar
and fir, where storks may nest.

You made the moon for season
and holy trumpet call,
the sunset and the darkness,
when forest creatures crawl;
the pride of lions hunting
together, for their prey,
and gathering in their dens, as
the sun brings on the day,
humanity, to labour
until the evening fall -
you made and feed creation,
the Father of us all.

How manifold the wildlife
in wisdom you create;
the earth is overflowing,
my Lord, from your estate:
the wide, majestic ocean,
where awesome things are found;
unfathomable numbers
of creeping things abound;
our ships upon the waters,
to voyage far away;
and, deep beneath the surface,
Leviathan at play.

They wait for you to feed them;
they gather in their food.
Your hand is ever open,
to fill them all with good.
You hide away your presence,
you leave them in dismay;
you gather up their spirits,
as dust and ash decay;
but, sending breath upon them,
to freshen and revive,
renewing your creation,
you make them live and thrive.

The glory of the Lord be
upon us evermore.
May God, the Lord, rejoice in
creation, and its store.
He turns his gaze towards us,
he looks across the earth,
which trembles in his presence,
acknowledges his worth.
The noble, lofty mountains,
before his touch and glance,
in smoke and fire erupting,
ignite at his advance.

My soul, sing praise, resounding
with joy in every breath,
to God my Lord above, till
the onset of my death,
and may the Lord accept me;
I contemplate him here.
May sinners all be banished
from earth, and disappear.
May those who practice evil
be finished off and die.
My soul, now bless the one, who
is God and Lord on high!

Psalm 105 without Alleluias
77 77
Monkland, Nottingham

Praise the Lord, invoke his name,
let the peoples know his fame.
Sing to him with sacred air,
weigh his wonders and his care.

Glorify his holy name,
let your joyful heart acclaim.
Trust the Lord, who will endure;
seek his face for evermore.

Heed the wonders he has done,
heed his judgements, every one,
seed of Abraham his slave,
Jacob's heirs he chose to save.

God, the Lord, proclaims, his care
by his judgements, everywhere,
calls to mind the oaths he swore
and commanded, evermore:

oaths with Abraham of old,
Isaac's covenant to uphold;
Jacob's statute evermore.
Israel's eternal law,

saying, 'I will now donate
Canaan's land, for your estate.'
They were few and very small,
dwelling there among them all.

As they wandered here and there,
crossing kingdoms everywhere,
none oppressed them in their wake;
kings were censured for their sake.

'Do not touch my sacred clans;
leave the prophets of my hands.'
Then he sent a famine down,
broke their livelihood around.

But he sent a man ahead;
Joseph, as a slave, was led,
fettered in unending pain,
round his neck, an iron chain.

Till the time of his reward,
he was tested by the Lord.
Pharaoh sent to set him free,
raised him from his low degree.

He was lord of everything;
Pharaoh made him like a king,
binding princes at his will,
making elders wiser still.

Israel, in Egypt, then
sojourned in the land Ham.
Jacob grew, in spite of woes,
far outnumbering all his foes.

God turned Egypt's heart away,
so they hated them that day,
planning ill against his folk,
laying down a bitter yoke.

But, from Levi, there were sent,
chosen servants of his tent,
Moses, as the voice of God,
Aaron, with the holy rod.

By his precepts, he began
wonders in the land of Ham,
sending darkness on their lords,
who rebelled against his words.

He made water into blood;
fish were dying in the flood.
Frogs were teeming everywhere,
every palace, every square.

Then he brought a swarm of flies,
over all the land and skies,
storms of furious hail for rain,
flaming fire in their terrain;

vine and fig and every tree,
splintering at his fierce decree,
while the locust, unrestrained,
devastated what remained.

Leaf and fruit and flower were doomed,
produce totally consumed.
In a night the firstborn died,
fruit of Egypt's youth and pride.

When he brought his people out,
none were seen to fall or shout;
with their silver and their gold,
every tribe was then enrolled.

Egypt boasted as they left;
terrified, they were bereft.
God protected Israel,
cloud and fire his place to dwell.

Then he brought them quails at even,
fed them with the bread of heaven.
Waters flowed across the sands,
sprung from rock in desert lands.

God had kept his holy plan,
which he swore to Abraham;
brought his chosen people out,
with exhilarating shout.

And he gave into their hands
all the toil of foreign lands,
so that they would keep his law,
guard his precepts evermore.

Psalm 105 with Alleluias
77 77 and Alleluias
Orientis Partibus

Praise the Lord, invoke his name,
let the peoples know his fame.
Sing to him with sacred air,
weigh his wonders and his care.
Alleluia.

Glorify his holy name,
let your joyful heart acclaim.
Trust the Lord, who will endure;
seek his face for evermore.
Alleluia.

Heed the wonders he has done,
heed his judgements, every one,
seed of Abraham his slave,
Jacob's heirs he chose to save.
Alleluia.

God, the Lord, proclaims, his care
by his judgements, everywhere,
calls to mind the oaths he swore
and commanded, evermore:
- Alleluia -

oaths with Abraham of old,
Isaac's covenant to uphold;
Jacob's statute evermore.
Israel's eternal law,
- Alleluia -

saying, 'I will now donate
Canaan's land, for your estate.'
They were few and very small,
dwelling there among them all.
Alleluia.

As they wandered here and there,
crossing kingdoms everywhere,
none oppressed them in their wake;
kings were censured for their sake.
Alleluia.

'Do not touch my sacred clans;
leave the prophets of my hands.'
Then he sent a famine down,
broke their livelihood around.
Alleluia.

But he sent a man ahead;
Joseph, as a slave, was led,
fettered in unending pain,
round his neck, an iron chain.
Alleluia.

Till the time of his reward,
he was tested by the Lord.
Pharaoh sent to set him free,
raised him from his low degree.
Alleluia.

He was lord of everything;
Pharaoh made him like a king,
binding princes at his will,
making elders wiser still.
Alleluia.

Israel, in Egypt, then
sojourned in the land Ham.
Jacob grew, in spite of woes,
far outnumbering all his foes.
Alleluia.

God turned Egypt's heart away,
so they hated them that day,
planning ill against his folk,
laying down a bitter yoke.
Alleluia.

But, from Levi, there were sent,
chosen servants of his tent,
Moses, as the voice of God,
Aaron, with the holy rod.
Alleluia.

By his precepts, he began
wonders in the land of Ham,
sending darkness on their lords,
who rebelled against his words.
Alleluia.

He made water into blood;
fish were dying in the flood.
Frogs were teeming everywhere,
every palace, every square.
Alleluia.

Then he brought a swarm of flies,
over all the land and skies,
storms of furious hail for rain,
flaming fire in their terrain;
- Alleluia -

vine and fig and every tree,
splintering at his fierce decree,
while the locust, unrestrained,
devastated what remained.
Alleluia.

Leaf and fruit and flower were doomed,
produce totally consumed.
In a night the firstborn died,
fruit of Egypt's youth and pride.
Alleluia.

When he brought his people out,
none were seen to fall or shout;
with their silver and their gold,
every tribe was then enrolled.
Alleluia.

Egypt boasted as they left;
terrified, they were bereft.
God protected Israel,
cloud and fire his place to dwell.
Alleluia.

Then he brought them quails at even,
fed them with the bread of heaven.
Waters flowed across the sands,
sprung from rock in desert lands.
Alleluia.

God had kept his holy plan,
which he swore to Abraham;
brought his chosen people out,
with exhilarating shout.
Alleluia.

And he gave into their hands
all the toil of foreign lands,
so that they would keep his law,
guard his precepts evermore.
Alleluia.

Psalm 106
88 88 D
Schmücke Dich

Praise the Lord for all his goodness,
constant love in all its fullness.
Who can tell the mighty story,
who proclaim your praise and glory?
Blessed are those who practice justice,
dealing constantly in fairness.
Lord, recall your congregation,
answer me in your salvation.

Look on us in your devotion,
so your people, who are chosen,
may rejoice in their confession,
glory here in your possession.
Like our forebears, with presumption,
we have sinned in our corruption,
who ignored your deeds in Egypt,
all your wonders in their conflict.

When they scorned his loving-kindness,
by the sea, rebelled in blindness,
he rebuked the sea, to save them,
covered those who had enslaved them,
led them through the mighty waters,
with their herds and sons and daughters,
so his name might be established,
and his greatness might be published.

Through the sea, as through a desert,
safe from bondage, he was shepherd,
as he drowned all their oppressors,
inundated their aggressors.
Then, with joyful celebration,
they believed his revelation,
but they soon forgot his action,
would not wait for his direction.

Their eternal Father fed them
in the desert, where he led them,
when their hunger was voracious,
uncontrollably rapacious.
Though they tried his toleration,
still he kept away starvation,
but, for all his benediction,
came a ruinous affliction.

Jealous, then they challenged Moses,
questioned Aaron, whom God chose as
priest, to serve the Lord before them,
offer blessing, and restore them.
So the earth devoured Dathan,
and the households of Abiram.
Fire consumed their congregation,
burned them as a vile oblation.

Horeb saw them cast an idol,
serve their golden calf, unbridled.
Revelling, they replaced his glory,
with an ox and empty story.
They forgot the God who saved them,
from Egyptians who enslaved them,
who in Ham performed a wonder,
rent the Sea of Reeds asunder.

God planned their extermination,
but for Moses at his station,
standing in the breach before him,
to placate him and implore him.
Even then they still rejected
pleasant lands the Lord selected.
They refused his affirmation,
that they were a holy nation.

In their camp they were bemoaning,
grumbling, murmuring and groaning.
Since they spurned the Lord's instruction,
he commanded their destruction,
putting forth his arm to slay them,
in the desert to delay them,
till they fell among the nations,
scattered in their congregations.

Then they honoured Baal of Peor,
trying God and his decree, for
they ate food of desecration;
there was ravenous contagion.
But, when Phinehas resisted,
and the pestilence desisted,
righteousness, by this increased, would
earn him everlasting priesthood.

Next, at Meribah they vexed him,
by the water they perplexed him,
so that even Moses suffered,
when he had become embittered.
They had made his soul contentious,
and his words were injudicious,
for they did not take the nations,
disobeyed his regulations.

Even worse, their foreign marriage
led them further, to disparage
God, the Lord, by serving idols,
snared in wickedness and rivals.
They were sacrificing children,
to the demons - even children! -
shedding sinless blood as water,
when they slew their son or daughter.

Since they had become profane, and
served the foreign gods of Canaan,
blood of consecrated infants
stained their land, and their existence.
Then the Lord, with indignation,
burned against their fornication.
He derided all their stations,
gave them over to the nations.

Subjugated by aggressors,
hateful foes, increasing pressures,
squeezing them to make them cower,
shaming them beneath their power,
he repeatedly delivered;
they were thoroughly bewildered,
fell, abased in their defiance,
evil counsel, and alliance.

When he saw their subjugation,
heard their cry of lamentation,
he recalled his oath before them,
constant love and favour for them.
He repented, their creator,
since his love was so much greater,
made their captors to have pity,
those who took them from their city.

Save us, Lord our God, collect us
from the nations, and protect us,
that we may proclaim your station,
holy name, and exaltation.
Blessed be God, the Lord of Israel,
for eternity without fail.
Let them answer, men and women,
'Amen. Alleluia. Amen.'

Psalm 107
98 98
St. Clement

Come, praise the Lord, our good proponent,
his loving mercy evermore.
Let those redeemed from their opponent
acknowledge that the Lord is sure.

Assembled from the foreign peoples,
from east and west and south and north,
astray in wilderness and evils,
they wandered, weary, back and forth.

They could not find a place to dwell in,
a city fit for their abode.
Through thirst and hunger strength was failing,
their soul was fainting on the road.

They sought the Lord in their vexation;
his hand delivered them from harm.
By him they reached their destination,
to open ways without alarm.

So let them praise the Lord for wonders,
his love and grace to humankind.
He satisfies the one who hungers,
with food and good of every kind.

Within their dark incarceration,
confined in deadly iron shade,
were those who spurned God's wise salvation,
who scorned the Most High Father's aid.

He overcame their soul with trouble;
they staggered, helpless in dismay.
Their hearts were prone to fall and stumble,
with no relief by night or day.

They sought the Lord in their vexation;
his hand delivered them from harm,
from bondage and incarceration,
from deadly shade to rest and calm.

So let them praise the Lord for wonders,
his love and grace to humankind.
He shatters doors of bronze, and sunders
the chains, in which they were confined.

When fools were lost in their transgression,
their souls abhorring any bread,
and sins were causing their oppression,
they trod the pathway to the dead.

They sought the Lord in their vexation;
his hand delivered them from harm.
He saved them from annihilation,
and sent his word with healing balm.

So let them praise the Lord for wonders,
his love and grace to humankind,
with praise and sacrifice in numbers,
proclaim and call his deeds to mind.

The folk who sail upon the ocean,
who earn their living on the quay,
have seen amazing things in motion,
the Lord at work upon the sea.

He spoke to raise a stormy tempest,
and lifted up the boiling wave.
Their churning, rolling, queasy progress
dissolved their souls, with none to save.

But reeling, staggering at their station,
like drunkards, helpless in alarm,
they sought the Lord in their vexation;
his hand delivered them from harm.

And by his word the storm abated;
he stilled the waves and boiling sea.
Their hearts at ease, their souls elated,
he led them to their longed-for quay.

So let them praise the Lord for wonders,
his love and grace to humankind,
exalt his name among the elders,
the congregation, all combined.

He makes the rivers dry and hostile,
the bubbling springs a thirsty ground.
A fruitful land becomes infertile,
if vile inhabitants are found.

He fills a desert waste with water,
a barren land with springing well.
He gives the hungry son or daughter
a city, where they safely dwell.

They sow their seed and plant their vineyards,
their fruit brings forth abundant yield,
their herds, increasing by their hundreds,
they multiply in every field.

They had been small and unimportant,
abused and bowed, with no relief,
beneath oppression lying dormant,
constrained by wickedness and grief.

He covers nobles with derision,
and makes them lost among the rocks,
transforming poor from low condition
to clans, as numerous as their flocks.

Let righteous people, all rejoicing,
consider this with one accord.
With evil stilled, their tongues are voicing
the loving mercies of the Lord.

Psalm 108

LM

Deus Tuorum Militum

O God, my heart will ever sing,
give praise and music to my King.
With lute and harp awake, to play
the glorious music of the day!

I praise the Lord with heart and voice;
among the peoples I rejoice,
to offer music for my King;
may all the nations hear me sing.

The heavenly powers magnify
your truth and grace, above the sky.
O God, let heaven proclaim your worth,
your glory over all the earth.

O God, arise, deliver now,
and save your treasure, here below.
Establish us, and give to me
an answer from your sanctuary.

'The land of Shechem I divide,
I measure Sukkoth in my pride.
Manasseh, Gilead - they are mine,
with Ephraim on my head to shine.

The land of Judah is a staff;
at Edom, Moab, I will laugh.
The Philistines will be afraid,
as I, with victory shout, invade.'

Will you, O God, engage the siege
of Edom, and invade the breach?
For you have left us on our own;
our armies go to war alone.

O be our saviour once again,
for human armies march in vain.
In God the soldiers overthrow,
for you will trample down the foe.

Psalm 109
DCM
First Mode Melody

God of my praise, do not ignore
abuse and ill deceit.
Raising their voice, an evil maw,
they falsify and cheat.
I am surrounded by their hate,
by their gratuitous war.
Scorning my love and prayer, they wait,
with ill and spite in store.

[Wicked opponents, bring them near
to cross-examine him.
Letting your verdict be severe,
his prayer be deemed a sin.
May someone else usurp his place,
and let his days be few,
making his wife and children face,
without him, all they do.

May they go wandering far for bread,
be driven from their soil.
Lenders exacting every thread,
may foreigners despoil.
May there be no-one, who will pay
attention to their need;
family and name be wiped away,
no children to succeed.

Brooding upon his mother's sin,
his fathers' old offence,
Lord, may their sins reside within
your mind and sight and sense.
Cut off his memory from the earth,
for he forgot to care,
driving the poor, in need and dearth,
to death in their despair.

Loving his curses, may a curse
oppress him every day.
Blessing to him was just perverse,
so take it far away.
Clothed in his nasty, vile abuse,
the covering which he owns,
seeping within, let ill infuse,
like oil, into his bones.

May it be like the clothes he wears,
the garments of his mirth;
may it be like the belt he bears
each day, around his girth.
All those who curse me or oppose,
the Lord will now control.
This is his recompense for those,
who speak against my soul.]

You though, O Lord, address my claim,
because your love is strong,
guarding the honour of your name;
deliver me from wrong.
I, who am low and poor within,
my heart is pierced today.
I am a shadow, drawn and thin,
a locust flung away.

Fasting has left me nearly dead;
my flesh is lean and lame.
All those who see me shake their head,
my life an open shame.
Help me, O Lord, my God above,
defend me by your hand.
Teach them to know your grace and love,
O Lord, and your command.

Bless, though they curse, and, when they rise,
let them be wrapped in blame.
May I rejoice at their demise,
disgrace and robe of shame.
Praising the Lord, I will adore,
within the faithful throng,
he who upholds the needy poor,
to save their soul from wrong.

Psalm 110
LM
Gonfalon Royal

The Lord has spoken to my lord,
'At my right hand, come, take your seat,
until I make the hateful foe
a lowly footstool for your feet.'

The Lord will send your righteous power
from Zion's royal, holy height,
to rule above the hateful foe,
receiving tribute in your might.

With holy splendour of the dawn,
your reign is like the new-born sun;
your kingdom shines in endless power
and glistening youth, to run and run.

The Lord himself has sworn an oath,
will not repent or hold in check,
you stand as my eternal priest,
according to Melchizedek.

My lord, our God at your right hand,
will shatter kings with furious might;
he judges all across the earth,
assessing nations in your sight.

He piles their corpses through the lands,
and shatters those who lie there dead.
Our king will drink beside the way,
to quench his thirst and raise his head.
Amen.

Psalm 111 (An Alphabetic Psalm)

78 78 and Alleluia
St. Albinus

All my heart will praise the Lord,
offering him my celebration,
boundless joy with one accord,
in the upright congregation.
Alleluia.

Champion over all, and great,
is the Lord in every action,
dear to those who watch and wait,
who acknowledge their attraction.
Alleluia.

Every deed of his is right,
honourable and full of splendour,
full of righteousness and might,
standing firm and strong forever.
Alleluia.

Gracious is the Lord alone,
merciful in his compassion.
His amazing deeds are known;
we remember every action.
Alleluia.

In his love he has assigned
food for all of those, who fear him.
Jealously, he keeps in mind
law and covenant, ever near him.
Alleluia.

Keen to show his mighty deeds,
he declared them to his nation.
Land from foreign powers proceeds
to our hand, by his donation.
Alleluia.

Marvellous are his deeds, and wise,
all his actions true and honest.
Noble deeds, before our eyes,
are unfailing, as he promised.
Alleluia.

Operations of his hand
are secure, and stand forever,
permanent at his command,
true and upright at his pleasure.
Alleluia.

Ransom for his people here,
he has wrought his great endeavour.
Since he made his covenant clear,
he commanded us forever.
Alleluia.

To the folk who fear the Lord,
he is honourable and holy,
undefiled in name and word,
he, the source of wisdom solely.
Alleluia.

Virtue follows all their days,
keeping watch as they obey him,
while his name and endless praise
stand for ever, as they pray him.
Alleluia.

Psalm 112 (An Alphabetic Psalm)
78 78 and Alleluia
St. Albinus

All who fear the Lord are blessed,
joyful in their celebrations.
Blamelessly they have confessed
pleasure in his regulations.
Alleluia.

Celebration is their strength,
passing on to their relations,
down the ages, when, at length,
they are blessed for generations.
Alleluia.

Exaltation lies at hand,
in their house a hoard of treasure,
for their righteousness will stand,
holding firm and sure forever.
Alleluia.

Glorious light is rising clear
in the darkness, for the gracious.
High and upright year by year,
they are merciful and righteous.
Alleluia.

It goes well for those who lend,
who are gracious in their dealings.
Justice ever will attend,
helping all their ways and feelings.
Alleluia.

Keeping firm, they never sway,
right and just in their endeavour.
Lasting memory ever stays;
noble names will live forever.
Alleluia.

Mindful that the Lord is near,
when they hear of ill prevailing,
none who trust in him will fear,
or will find their heart is failing.
Alleluia.

Often, though they are afraid,
faithful hearts will be supported.
Plainly they will see displayed
all their adversaries thwarted.
Alleluia.

Reaching out, they lend a hand
to the needy, who implore them,
so their righteousness will stand,
firm forever, still before them.
Alleluia.

Their posterity will rise,
glorious in their exaltation.
Unrepentant, wicked eyes
contemplate it with vexation.
Alleluia.

Vainly they will know despair,
grinding teeth in their confusion.
When their evil passions flare,
they will perish in delusion.
Alleluia.

Psalm 113
88 88 89
Surrey

Come praise, you servants of the Lord,
give honour to his holy name,
the Lord, for evermore adored,
for all eternity the same.
From east to west, in lands afar,
the Lord is worshipped. Alleluia.

The Lord is high above the earth,
more glorious than the spheres or sky.
The Lord our God, of matchless worth,
establishes his throne on high,
who stoops to view the shooting star,
the earth and mortals. Alleluia.

God lifts the poor from underground,
he raises beggars from the slums.
They live with nobles all around,
and eat their fill, instead of crumbs.
He gives a home to those, who are
alone and childless. Alleluia.

Psalm 114
65 65 65 75
Dun Aluinn

When we came from Egypt,
from a foreign land,
Judah was his temple,
Israel his command;
then the sea retreated,
Jordan fled away,
peaks arose as leaping rams,
hills as lambs at play.

Why, you sea, retreat, or,
Jordan, fly away,
peaks, as leaping rams, or,
hills, as lambs at play?
Let the earth recoil and
writhe before our King.
Rock he makes a gushing well,
flint he makes a spring.

Psalm 115
87 87 D
Lux Eoi

Not to us, Lord, not to us, but
glory to your name on high,
full of truth and loving kindness,
full of victory when we cry.
Why is every nation asking,
'How can God be there at all?'
God is reigning high in heaven,
finding joy in great and small.

Gold or silver human idols,
empty works of mortal mind,
never speaking, never sensing,
never breathing, deaf and blind,
never walking, vain and voiceless,
dead to sense and sight and sound -
cold and lifeless are their makers,
soulless, in devotion bound.

House of Israel, house of Aaron,
all whose faith is in the Lord,
trusting in the help of God, who
is our shield and great reward,
God remembers us forever,
all the faithful, great and small.
House of Israel, house of Aaron,
God will bless us, one and all.

May the Lord increase his blessing,
bless you and your seed from birth,
blessed together, by the maker
of the sky and sea and earth.
Though the dead and silent spirits
never praise the Lord above,
we will pour eternal blessing
to the Lord, the God of love.

Psalm 116
66 66 88
Love Unknown

Lord, you have heard my prayer,
when grief and death surround,
when Sheol's cords ensnare
my soul, and I am bound.
I love you, Lord, with every breath,
for you have set me free from death.

Calling upon his name,
I said, 'Come, save my soul!'
He saves the low from blame,
and makes the simple whole.
Turn back, my soul, when you are pressed;
the Lord has fully brought you rest.

He saves from hell below,
from tears when overawed,
my feet from stumbling, so
I live before the Lord,
Our God is gracious, he is just,
and in his mercy we will trust.

When I was so oppressed,
I thought that I would die,
and in alarm confessed
the human race a lie.
I pay my vows for saving grace;
I drink his cup, and seek his face.

Precious before the Lord,
the deaths of those who fear,
while I fulfil my word,
before his people here.
Lord, I will serve, was born a slave,
but you release my bonds, to save.

Thanks I will offer now,
call on his name in fear,
while I fulfil my vow,
before his people here.
Within his house, by all adored,
Jerusalem, O praise the Lord.

Psalm 117
4664
Plaisir d'amour

O praise the Lord,
all peoples of the earth;
let all the world acclaim.
O praise the Lord.

O praise the Lord,
whose love to us is great,
whose truth will never end.
O praise the Lord.

Psalm 118
87 87 D
Golden Sheaves

Come, praise the Lord, for he is good;
his kindness is forever.
Let Israel say, 'For he is good;
his kindness is forever.'
Let all the house of Aaron say,
'His kindness is forever.'
Let those who fear the Lord now say,
'His kindness is forever.'

My prayer from ill rose to the Lord,
and he responded clearly.
In spacious pasturage abroad
he settled me securely.
The Lord beside, I never quail
at mortal degradation.
The Lord beside, I never pale
at hateful confrontation.

Far better now to seek the Lord
than trust in human beings.
Far better now to seek the Lord
than trust in noble dealings.
To cries of praise he saves the just,
with mighty hand in power;
his mighty hand will raise the crushed,
a mighty hand in power.

The nations all surrounded me,
but in his name I break them,
surrounded, yes, surrounded me,
and in his name I break them.
They circle round, like angry bees,
a thorny, blazing mayhem,
but I extinguish them with ease,
when in his name I break them.

You drove me to the brink of death;
the Lord was there to aid me,
my song and strength with every breath,
to liberate and save me.
I will survive to live and tell
his mighty operation;
with discipline he taught me well,
and freed me from damnation.

Unbar the gates of righteousness,
that here I may acclaim him.
This is the gate the Lord has blessed;
the righteous will proclaim him.
All thanks to you for you replied,
became my sure salvation,
my Ancient One, my praise and guide,
my God and exaltation.

The stone the builders all denied
is now the one foundation.
This action, by the Lord supplied,
became our inspiration.
This is the day the Lord has made;
we celebrate your splendour,
so prosper with your mighty aid,
and save us, our defender.

Blessed is the one who comes from God;
from heaven's court we bless you.
His glory shines with lightning rod,
while worshippers process to
his holy place, of stone and wood,
his temple here forever.
Come, praise the Lord, for he is good;
his kindness is forever.

Psalm 119.1-8
CM
St. Peter

Aleph
All those whose way is sound are blessed,
who guard the Lord's decrees,
and seek his charge with all their heart,
yes, they will walk with ease.

All those who do no wicked deed
will follow in his ways,
and you command that we should keep
your precepts all our days.

Ah now, if only all my ways
were firm in your demands,
and then I would not be ashamed,
when viewing your commands.

As I have learned with upright heart
to praise you for your laws;
accept me, Lord, for I will keep
your statutes, every clause.

Psalm 119.9-16
CM
Song 67

Beth
But how shall youthful ones be clean,
to heed your word and way?
Because I truly seek your law,
O never let me stray.

Because my heart has stored your words,
I keep myself from sin.
Before my eyes, Lord, you are blessed;
implant your rules within.

Bar none, my lips have told of each
commandment in your law.
Before me all your charges are
a glorious wealth and store.

By musing on your precepts, I
will look for you today.
By savouring all your statutes, I
recall your words and way.

Psalm 119.17-24
CM
Metzler's Redhead

Gimel
Completely care for me, that I
may keep your words in store;
correct my eyes that I may live,
to see your awesome law.

Conceal no longer your commands
from me, a stranger here.
Continual longing for your law
consumes my soul in fear.

Contempt and cursing follow those,
who stray from your commands.
Command that they be rolled away;
I keep your law's demands.

Conniving princes sit and smear;
I muse on your demand,
content that all your charges are
my counsel and command.

Psalm 119.25-32
CM
Abridge

Daleth
Deliver me from dust and death;
your word is my support.
Direct me in your statutes, Lord;
you answer my report.

Disclose your precepts, as I muse
on all your wonders, Lord.
Despair and grief depress my soul;
confirm me by your word.

Disable falsehood by your law;
give grace to me, my Lord.
Depending on your just commands,
I hold your faithful word.

Do not put me to shame, O Lord;
I cling to your commands.
Discharging your decrees, my heart
is full of your demands.

Psalm 119.33-40
CM
London New

He
Explain your statutes, Lord, to me,
so I may guard your way.
Encourage me to know your law
entirely day by day.

Escort me in the path of your
commands I have adored.
Enthuse my heart for your decrees,
and not for violent fraud.

Entice my eyes from worthless things;
revive me in your way.
Enact your promise to your slave,
so I may fear and pray.

Eject reproaches which I fear;
your laws reward my soul.
Enliven me in righteousness;
your precepts are my goal.

Psalm 119.41-48
CM
Stockton

Waw
Fulfil in me your saving word,
your loving-mercies, Lord.
For I will answer those who scorn;
I trust your skilful word.

Fixated on your judgements, Lord,
O let me speak the truth.
Forthwith I fully keep your law,
forever from my youth.

For I have sought your precepts, as
I walk about at large.
Forthwith I boldly speak to kings,
and tell them of your charge.

For I delight myself within,
and love all your demands.
Forthwith I lift my hands in love,
and muse on your commands.

Psalm 119.49-56
CM
Southwell (Irons)

Zayin
Give, Lord, the word for which I long;
remember it for me:
great is my comfort in distress,
revived by your decree.

Grotesque abuse I undergo;
I keep your word for sure.
Great is my comfort, as I call
to mind your timeless law.

Grim wickedness enrages me,
when they forsake your way.
Glad are the songs your rules inspire,
wherever I may stay.

Gestating on your law at night,
I call to mind your name,
great are your precepts, Lord; I guard
your everlasting claim.

Psalm 119.57-64
CM
Belmont

Heth
Habitually I keep your words;
you are my portion, Lord.
Hear all my heartfelt pleas to you;
be gracious by your word.

Here now I turn toward your charge,
reviewing all my way.
Haste drives me on to your commands;
I never go astray.

Horrendous snares surround, but I
remember your demands.
Here in the night I give you thanks,
for all your just commands.

Harmoniously I live with those,
who keep your precepts near.
How full the earth is, Lord, with grace;
O make your statutes clear.

Psalm 119.65-72
CM
Solomon

Teth
I know that all your works are good,
according to your word.
Impart your knowledge by your laws;
I trust and keep them, Lord.

I went astray when in distress,
but now I keep your word.
In doing good your goodness shines,
so teach your statutes, Lord.

Ignoring their abuse and lies,
I keep your precepts close.
I find your law delights my heart,
while theirs, like fat, are gross.

In my affliction, it was good
to learn your statutes, Lord.
I know your law is richer than
a gold or silver hoard.

Psalm 119.73-80
CM
Richmond

Yodh
Just as you made me firm to learn,
and fathom your commands,
joy fills all those who see and fear;
I long for your demands.

Justice becomes my burden, Lord,
but you are firm above.
Just like the words that you command,
O comfort me with love.

Just let compassion make me live;
your law is my delight.
Just shame each violent witness here,
by precepts in my sight.

Join me to those who fear your name,
that they may know your laws,
just as my heart is unashamed
to keep them, every clause.

Psalm 119.81-88
CM
Beatitudo

Kaph
Know how my soul and eyes are spent,
seeking your just decree.
Keep me still faithful to your word;
when will you comfort me?

Kept as a wineskin in the smoke,
I will recall your ways.
Kill all my foes by your commands;
how many are my days?

Know how the insolent have dug
illegal snares for me.
Keep me from lying charges, since
your laws are fair and free.

Know how they nearly took my life,
as I obeyed your laws.
Keep me alive, so, by your grace,
I hold them, every clause.

Psalm 119.89-96
CM
St. Fulbert

Lamedh
Long-live your word in heaven above,
my Lord, to reassure.
Long-live the earth which you have made,
established and secure.

Legitimate, they stand this day,
with all in your employ.
Lost in my pain I perish, if
your law were not my joy.

Long-live your precepts in my mind;
by them you give me life.
Let me be yours and save me, for
I sought them in my strife.

Licentious folk desire my harm,
but I will know your charge.
Long have I known that your commands
exceed the world at large.

Psalm 119.97-104
CM
Stracathro

Mem
My constant meditation here,
I love to choose your way.
More wisdom from your law is mine,
than foes who go astray;

more prudence than my teachers, for
your precepts are my thought;
more knowledge than my elders, since
I keep them as I ought.

My feet refrain from evil ways,
that I may keep your word.
May I remain within your laws,
since you have taught me, Lord.

Much sweeter than the honeycomb,
your laws are to my taste.
My knowledge of your word, makes me
abhor the false and base.

Psalm 119.105-112
CM
Martyrdom

Nun
Nearby your word will light my path,
and shine before my feet.
Now I confirm and swear to keep
your righteous laws complete.

Necessities afflicted me;
revive me by your word.
New offerings graciously receive;
impart your laws, O Lord.

Not failing to recall your law,
my soul is in your hand.
Nor even wicked snares can make
me err from your command.

Now all your charges, Lord, will be
a joyful gift to me.
Near to your statutes I incline
my heart continually.

Psalm 119.113-120
CM
Albano

Samekh
Obtuse and feeble ones I hate;
I love your law and word.
Obediently I wait for you,
my shield and shelter, Lord.

O turn from me, you wicked folk;
I guard my God's commands.
O help me live, Lord, unashamed,
in line with your demands.

O keep me safe, to contemplate
your statutes night and day.
Outside your rules are those who lie;
you toss them all away.

Opposing wicked folk as dross,
your charge is very dear.
O how I tremble for your laws;
my flesh is cold from fear.

Psalm 119.121-128
CM
Dundee

'Ayin
Preserve me from oppression; I
fulfil your righteous law.
Provide your guarantee for good;
let no contempt endure.

Pursuing just and saving words,
my eyes are worn away.
Perform your love for me, and teach
me all your rules today.

Provide your wisdom to your slave,
to know your whole decree.
Promote your law at once, O Lord,
on those who disagree.

Preferring your commandments, more
than gold, the finest prize,
preferring all your precepts, I
detest the way of lies.

Psalm 119.129-136
CM
St. James

Pe
Remarkable are your decrees;
my soul keeps your command.
Resplendence from your charges helps
the simple understand.

Respiring as I long for your
commands, I will proclaim.
Regard me justly by your grace,
with those who love your name.

Restore my steps by all your speech;
from evil keep me free.
Redeem me from abuse, so I
may keep your just decree.

Regard me with your glorious face;
O teach me your demands.
Reduced to tears, I mourn that they
do not keep your commands.

Psalm 119.137-144
CM
Tallis's Ordinal

Tsadhe
Sincerity and righteousness
form all your judgements, Lord;
secure and faithful are your law,
your charge and upright word.

Since hateful foes ignore your words,
my zeal consumes my soul.
Sublime and pure is all your speech;
I love its kind control.

Small is my lot, abhorred, but I
do not forget your law;
secure and right, your precepts are
the truth for evermore.

Surrounding me are strain and stress;
your charge is my delight.
so make me know your just commands,
to live within your sight.

Psalm 119.145-152
CM
St. Botolph

Qoph
To you I call with all my heart;
Lord, answer me and save,
that I may keep your charges well,
the statutes, which you gave.

Toward the dawn I rise to cry;
I wait upon your word.
Throughout the night I wake, to muse
on all your speech, my Lord.

Then hear my voice in love; revive
me, by your laws today.
Though near to me, my foes are far
from you, and from your way.

Truth rests in all of your commands,
and you, my Lord, are near.
The charges, which you gave of old,
will stand forever here.

Psalm 119.153-160
CM
St. Magnus

Resh
Unshackle me from desperate need;
I call to mind your way.
Uphold my cause, redeem me by
your word, to live today.

Unrighteous ones, who do not seek
your ways, will not be freed.
Uphold my life in kindness, Lord,
by laws you have decreed.

Unnumbered are my hateful foes;
I hold to your decrees.
Unfaithful ones ignore your speech;
I hate all such as these.

Uphold my life in mercy; look
and see, I love your word.
Unending righteousness and truth
sum up your precepts, Lord.

Psalm 119.161-168
CM
St. Stephen

Shin
Vindictive princes hound me, but
my heart fears your decree.
Vivaciously I celebrate,
as spoil, your speech to me.

Vile are their lies to me, and foul;
I love each law and clause.
View every day my sevenfold praise
of all your righteous laws.

Vast is their peace, who love your law,
no hindrance in their way.
Vouchsafe my hope, O Lord; I keep
your statutes all the day.

View how I keep your charges, how
I love them, every word.
View all my ways before you, as
I keep your precepts, Lord.

Psalm 119.169-176
CM
St. Flavian

Taw
Would that my cry came near your place;
O give me wisdom, Lord.
Would that my plea came to your face;
O save me by your word.

Would that my lips give praise, as you
impart all your demands.
Would that my tongue could sing your speech,
for all your just commands.

Would that your hand might give me help;
I choose your precepts, Lord.
Within I long for your release,
delighting in your word.

Would that my soul might live to praise;
your judgements help me stay.
When straying, Lord, bring back your sheep,
for I recall your way.

Psalm 120
65 65 and Refrain
Make Peace

Lord, in time of trouble,
I will make my prayer.
Save me from the liars;
treacherous tongues, beware!
Woe to me, that I sojourn in Meshech!
Woe to me, that my tent lies in Kedar!

How will you be answered,
treacherous, lying souls? -
arrows, burning, sharpened,
tempered in the coals.
Woe to me, that I sojourn in Meshech!
Woe to me, that my tent lies in Kedar!

Far too long I suffer
enemies of peace.
When I speak of concord,
they just never cease.
Woe to me, that I sojourn in Meshech!
Woe to me, that my tent lies in Kedar!

Psalm 121
66 86 SM
Franconia

I look towards the hills;
can they bring help to birth?
My help comes from the Lord himself,
who made the heaven and earth.

He will not let you slide,
your keeper will not sleep,
for Israel's Lord will never tire,
who has us in his keep.

The Lord will keep you safe,
the Lord will be your shade.
Of sun or moon or deadly curse
you need not be afraid.

The Lord will keep your soul,
from evil at your door.
The Lord will keep you day by day,
both now and evermore.

Psalm 122
LM
Herongate

How I rejoiced that we should go,
to see the temple of the Lord!
And now our feet are standing here,
Jerusalem, within your ward.

Jerusalem, a city built,
and altogether unified;
in her the thrones of judgement, for
the house of David, still reside.

The tribes of Israel ascend,
his tribes ascending to the Lord,
according to his covenant here,
to praise his name with one accord.

So pray prosperity and peace,
for those who love Jerusalem;
in citadel and hall be peace,
prosperity in all of them.

To friend and neighbour I will say,
The peace of God rest in your doors!
And, from the temple of the Lord,
may goodness come to you and yours.

Psalm 123
55 88 55
Arnstadt (Seelenbräutigam)

I will raise my eye
to your throne on high.
As the eye of slave to owner,
or of maid to those who own her,
so we seek the Lord,
for his gracious word.

I will raise my eye
to your throne on high.
God, be gracious, Lord, be gracious;
we are tired of those vexatious
mockers, who deride
in their scorn and pride.

Psalm 124
776 778
Innsbruck

Had God the Lord now failed us,
when hateful foes assailed us,
may Israel describe,
their anger would have burned us,
if God the Lord had spurned us,
they would have swallowed us alive.

Had God the Lord disowned us,
the waters would have drowned us,
may Israel now say,
their torrents would have flooded,
our souls they would have flooded,
the waters would have raged away.

So blessed be God the Lord, who
has not made us a prey to
their teeth, in war or dearth,
who breaks their snare and power,
our rescue from the fowler,
creator of the heaven and earth.

Psalm 125
66 66 44 44
Harewood

All those who trust the Lord
are firm as Zion's hill.
Jerusalem - the Lord
surrounds her people still,
surrounds her store
with mountain hold,
from days of old
for evermore.

The rod of wicked folk
will never rule in power,
on any righteous yoke,
in righteous home or tower,
lest upright souls
should turn their hands
to evil plans,
or wicked goals.

The Lord be good to all,
who live their upright lives;
but those who turn and fall
to evil, crooked drives,
the Lord propel
them far away,
so peace may stay
on Israel.

Psalm 126
87 87 D
Deerhurst

When the Lord established Zion
we were living in a dream.
Then our mouth was filled with laughter,
and our tongue with joyful theme.
Then they said, among the nations,
'All their Lord has done is great!'
Yes, our Lord does great things for us;
we rejoice and celebrate.

Re-establish us, our Lord, as
watercourses of the south.
Those who sow in tears and mourning
will return with joyful mouth.
Those who scatter seed in sorrow
come with sheaves in joyful state,
since our Lord does great things for us;
we rejoice and celebrate.

Psalm 127
87 87 D
Ode to Joy

If the Lord were not the builder
then the builders work in vain.
If he did not keep the city,
then the keepers watch in vain,
vain to wake and rise so early,
working hard and late to rest,
for to those who love and serve him
he gives sleep, in peace possessed.

Children of the womb are from the
Lord, his liberality,
as the arrows of a warrior,
seed of our vitality.
Blessed are those with quiver full,
their children standing, tall and straight.
They will not be shamed, and they will
answer foes within the gate.

Psalm 128
85 85 and Refrain
Guiting Power

Blessed are those who fear the Lord, who
walk within his ways.
Food is yours as your reward; you
prosper all your days.
Thus are blessed who fear the Lord,
with peace restored
to Israel.

You will have a wife to cherish,
like a fruitful vine;
children, like the olive, flourish
round you as you dine.
Thus are blessed who fear the Lord,
with peace restored
to Israel.

May the Lord from Zion bless you,
bless you all your days.
May your children's children bless you,
be your joy and praise.
May Jerusalem's reward
be peace restored
to Israel.

Psalm 129
76 76 D
Thornbury

How frequently they pressed me,
let Israel concede,
yes, from my youth they pressed me,
but they did not succeed.
They ploughed across my back, and
they made their furrows long,
but God the Lord is righteous,
who cuts the cords of wrong.

Let those with hate for Zion
be shamed and turned away,
be like the rooftop grasses,
that wither and decay,
which nobody can gather
into a harvest hoard,
and no-one offers blessing,
'We bless you by the Lord!'

Psalm 130
DCM
Third Mode Melody

Within the deep I cry to you;
my Lord, in mercy hear.
Lord, be attentive to my need,
and when I pray, give ear.
If you recorded human wrong,
my Lord, who would be cleared?
But you are gracious, you forgive,
and so you are revered.

My longing soul in patience waits;
I wait upon his word.
As watchers look toward the dawn,
my soul hopes in the Lord.
O Israel, look to the Lord,
whose saving love is strong,
for he will ransom Israel
from every kind of wrong.

Psalm 131
10 10
Song 46

Lord, I am free from lofty heart or eye;
let wonders and their greatness pass me by.

Within my soul is calm, in peace, at rest,
an infant child upon *his* mother's breast.

My infant soul is sleeping at my breast.
The Lord be Israel's hope, forever blessed.

Psalm 132
13 13 13 13 13 13
Thaxted

Remember, Lord, for David
the hardship he endured,
the vow he swore before you,
O Jacob's mighty Lord.
'I will not enter quickly
my house, or go to bed,
allow my eyes to slumber,
or lay my weary head,
until I find a place for
the sanctuary of the Lord,
the mighty one of Jacob,
where he may be adored.'

We heard it in Ephrathah,
we found it in the weald,
so let us go to worship
within his holy field,
to bow before his footstool,
his mighty ark of grace.
May Lord, with ark, ascend to
his holy resting place;
with righteousness for clothing,
let faithful priests give praise,
and David, your anointed,
attend you all his days.

The Lord has sworn to David,
and never will disown.
'The offspring you beget will
sit firmly on your throne.
If they will keep my charges,
my covenant and my law,
their issue and descendants
shall reign for evermore.'
For Zion is the Lord's, as
his chosen throne and seat,
the place of his desire, and
a footstool for his feet.

'This is my seat forever,
the place of my desire;
her poor will know abundance,
whatever they require.
With righteousness for clothing,
her priests give faithful praise;
I make a horn for David,
to flourish all his days.
A lamp for my anointed
I place, to shine and glow.
His foes will be ashamed, but
his crown will bloom and grow.'

Psalm 133
78 78 88
Liebster Jesu

How delectable and good -
unity and warm affection,
like the oil as Aaron stood,
for anointing and election,
purest oil on head descending,
over beard and robes extending!

How delectable and good -
unity and warm affection,
as the dew of Hermon's wood,
falling on the hills of Zion!
There the Lord commanded blessing,
endless life and health expressing.

Psalm 134
LM
Tallis's Canon

Come, all you servants of the Lord,
come, raise your hands and bless the Lord,
who stand by night within his place,
come, bless the Lord before his face.

Come, all you servants of the Lord,
come, raise your hands and bless the Lord.
The Lord from Zion bless you here,
who made the earth and starry sphere.

Psalm 135
66 66
St. Cecilia

Give praises to the Lord,
give praises to his name,
you servants of the Lord,
make music and acclaim.

Give praises to the Lord,
who stand within his place,
within the house of God,
whose name is full of grace.

Above each god and throne,
the Lord is good and great,
for Jacob is his own,
and Israel his estate.

Whatever his delight,
the Lord will bring to birth,
the seas, abyss and light,
in heaven and in the earth.

The mist from shore to shore,
the lightning with the rain,
the wind within his store -
they come from his domain.

He struck their firstborn dead
in Egypt's heart and coast.
He brought his signs and dread
on Pharaoh and his host.

He struck their nations down,
and slew, with mighty hand,
the kings who lived around
in kingdoms of the land.

He struck King Sihon down,
and every Amorite,
King Og with Bashan's crown,
and every Canaanite.

He took away their land,
a present for his race,
a portion from his hand,
for Israel, by his grace.

O Lord, your name is great,
a token all embrace.
You judge us, your estate;
have mercy on your race.

The idols of the lands,
of silver or of gold,
are wrought by human hands,
or poured into a mould.

They have no sight and, bound,
their mouth can give no cry,
their ear can hear no sound,
they give no breath or sigh.

Their makers will become,
like them, a senseless crowd,
and those, who still succumb
to idols, will be cowed.

So bless him, Israel's host,
and bless him, Aaron's ward;
the Lord be Levi's boast,
with those who fear his word.

The Lord be blessed by them.
May Zion bless the Lord.
In all Jerusalem,
may all now bless the Lord.

Psalm 136
6 6 6 D
Laudes Domini

Give thanks before the Lord,
his goodness be adored.
Forever is his love!
Give thanks before our God,
the God of every god.
Forever is his love!

Give thanks before the Lord,
the Lord of every lord.
Forever is his love!
He makes his wonders known,
his marvels, his alone,
Forever is his love!

He made the heaven and height,
with wisdom and with might.
Forever is his love!
He hammered out the land,
held back the sea with sand.
Forever is his love!

He made the lights on high,
the sun to rule the sky.
Forever is his love!
The moon and stars at night,
they rule the sky with light.
Forever is his love!

In Egypt there was dread;
he struck their firstborn dead.
Forever is his love!
He brought out Israel
from where they used to dwell.
Forever is his love!

His mighty arm and hand
were stretched across the land.
Forever is his love!
He cut the sea in two;
he led his people through.
Forever is his love!

They saw his mighty deeds
beside the Sea of Reeds.
Forever is his love!
He shattered Pharaoh's host,
cast up along the coast.
Forever is his love!

He guided Israel
through wilderness and hell.
Forever is his love!
He slaughtered mighty kings,
he slew majestic kings.
Forever is his love!

He struck King Sihon down,
King Og with Bashan's crown.
Forever is his love!
He slaughtered Amorites,
he slaughtered Canaanites.
Forever is his love!

He took away their land,
a portion from his hand.
Forever is his love!
His servant Israel
received a place to dwell.
Forever is his love!

He called to mind our dearth,
our hardship here on earth.
Forever is his love!
He saved us from our foes,
and all who would oppose.
Forever is his love!

He feeds the human race,
with sustenance and grace.
Forever is his love!
Give thanks to God above,
the ancient God of love.
Forever is his love!

Psalm 137
494 89 94
The Infant King

In Babylon,
there we sat down and wept for Zion,
in Babylon.
As for our harps we hung them high,
strung on the poplars of the marshes,
silent, as we remembered Zion,
in Babylon.

In Babylon,
there our tormentors asked for singing,
in Babylon.
'Sing us a joyful song from home.'
How can we sing a song of Zion,
sing of the Lord with strangers, aching,
in Babylon?

In Babylon,
if I forget Jerusalem, here
in Babylon,
may my right arm and tongue decay,
if I do not recall you, make you
first of my joys, Jerusalem, here
in Babylon.

[In Babylon,
call to mind Edom's generation,
in Babylon,
Lord, how Jerusalem was razed,
how they said, 'Raze her, lay her bare, and
down to the ground, to her foundation!'
In Babylon.

In Babylon,
Babylon's daughter, spoiled, behold her
in Babylon!
Blessed is the one who will repay,
dealing with you as you deserve, and
smashing your babes against a boulder!
In Babylon!]

Psalm 138
11 10 11 10 11 10 11 12
Londonderry Air

I give you praise, O Lord, with all my being;
before the gods I sing to you above.
I bow towards your holy temple, freeing
my praise of you, your name and truth and love.
Since you have glorified your great position,
your name and word of truth, from pole to pole,
and when I called you answered my petition,
you made me strong and bold within my heart and soul.

Let all the monarchs of the earth acclaim you,
give praise, O Lord, to you and to your name;
since they have heard of you, they will proclaim you,
your word of truth, the greatness of your fame.
Now let them sing that all your ways are holy,
that you, O Lord, are great and glorified.
The Lord is high, but notices the lowly;
he looks disdainfully upon our human pride.

Although my troubles press and make me cower,
you will preserve me, you restore my life.
Before my enemies you send your power,
your mighty arm, to save me in my strife.
The Lord will act for me with full endeavour,
fulfilling all his will upon the earth.
O Lord, your loving-kindness is forever,
do not abandon us, the folk you bring to birth.

Psalm 139
DCM
Coe Fen

Lord, you have searched me through and through,
you know me, where I stay,
when I rise up, and all I do,
my plans, from far away.
Proving me as I roam and rest,
you know me as a friend;
never a word have I expressed,
but you, Lord, comprehend.

You are before, you are behind,
you hold me in your hand.
Knowledge like this is undefined,
too high to understand.
How can I flee you? Where to go,
for you are everywhere?
Heaven above and hell below -
yes, you, Lord, you are there.

If, on the wings of dawn, I fly,
or live beyond the sea,
yes, even there you are near by,
to guide and set me free.
Darkness may cover where I stay,
the light be turned to night;
nightfall to you is as the day,
the darkness as the light.

You, Lord, you made my inward parts,
you wove me in the womb,
forming my limbs with fearful arts
below, in earth and gloom,
secretly weaving every bone,
with wonders hard to tell;
nothing is hidden, all is known,
and I, I know it well.

You saw my unborn members grow,
and all are written down;
all of my days were formed below
by you, and all are found.
Precious and numerous are your plans,
O Father of the Years,
countless as grains of shifting sands,
or stars within the spheres.

[God, how I wish that you would slay
deceitful, bloody spies.
Banish the rebels, turn away
the folk, who offer lies.
Do I not hate and loathe all those,
who rise to hate you, Lord?
Hatred has turned them into foes,
and hate is their reward.]

You are my Father of the Years;
I praise you through and through.
When I awake you calm my fears,
for I am still with you.
Search me to try my heart and mind,
for trouble or dismay;
lead me from pain, that I may find
your everlasting way.

Psalm 140
87 87 87
Oriel

Save me, Lord, from evil servants,
guard me from their violent hand,
from their earnest, evil purpose,
daily warfare of their plans,
bladed tongues as poisonous serpents,
vipers, eating dust and sand.

Keep me, Lord, from wicked powers,
guard me from their cruel pretence.
They prepare their traps for hours,
to ensnare me in events,
boasting pride, preparing wires,
making sure their vile intents.

Lord, you are my ancient Father;
listen to my earnest cry,
shelter on the day of slaughter,
strong salvation, Lord on high.
Do not let the wicked further
their desire or evil eye.

Circling lips, that mutter trouble,
will be covered in your ire.
Scattered coals and burning rubble
cast upon them, from your fire.
Deep in pits you pay them double,
sinking down into the mire.

Vile abuse and defamation
will not linger or succeed.
Lord, I know that exaltation
comes from you, for those in need.
Righteous ones, in veneration,
dwell secure, when you give heed.

Psalm 141

98 98
St. Clement

O Lord, I call within your presence;
give ear, come quickly when I sing,
my prayer, ascending as the incense,
my hands, an offering to my King.

Protect my lips and mouth, when speaking,
refrain my heart from evil sights,
from wanton dealing, or partaking
with wicked folk in their delights.

But let the righteous folk appoint me
a kind rebuke, for my misdeeds,
and let not sinners' oil anoint me;
I pray against their evil deeds.

Their judges, overthrown, and broken
against a rock within the land,
when my delightful words are spoken,
will hear them well, and understand.

Our bones, before the mouth of Sheol,
lie ploughed and cast upon the ground.
I look to you; do not reveal
my soul, but keep your hand around.

Protect me, Lord, from trap and toil,
from wicked folk, who strain and pry,
but let their nets and snares recoil,
while I, alone, go safely by.

Psalm 142
LM
Hereford

Before the Lord, in my constraint,
before the Lord, I plead for grace,
declare my anguish in complaint,
and seek in my distress his face.

For when my spirit faints inside,
you know my path, yes, you control,
while folk with hatred, as they hide,
are laying snares to take my soul.

Take note, at my right hand, behold,
for there is no-one who will care;
escape is dying in my soul,
no hope or refuge anywhere.

I cry to you, O Lord, in strife,
declare that you are my release.
Among the living you are life,
my joy, my holy lot and peace.

Attend to me, my cry resounds,
for I am low, and cannot flee.
Deliver me from those who hound,
my foes who are too strong for me.

Release me, so I may revere
your name, beyond my prison cell.
When righteous folk are gathering near,
then you will ever treat me well.

Psalm 143
776 778
Innsbruck

O Lord, in justice hear me,
give ear to truth, and clear me;
to you I pray for grace.
Do not bring me to sentence,
for, even with repentance,
not one can stand before your face.

My enemy pursues me;
they trample and abuse me;
they place me with the dead.
In darkness, where they bring me,
my spirit faints within me,
my heart appalled, and full of dread.

Recalling former ages,
your works and all their stages,
I contemplate your deeds.
I spread my hands towards you;
a weary land before you,
my soul is fainting in my need.

O Lord, make haste to hear me,
to answer and to clear me,
before my final breath.
Do not ignore my crying,
lest I be like the dying,
descending to the pit of death.

But may I hear at daybreak
your mercy, for your name's sake;
I put my trust in you.
So teach me, I implore you,
the way to walk before you;
I lift my pleading soul to you.

Lord, save me from detractors,
preserve me from attackers;
Lord, teach me all your will.
So may your spirit guide me,
on level ground, to hide me,
for you, my God, are present still.

[In righteousness revive me,
when troubles are beside me,
preserve your holy name.
In mercy slay my rivals,
who grieve my soul with trials,
for I am yours, to serve your fame.]

Psalm 144
77 77 D and Refrain
Mendelssohn

Blessed be God, the Lord, my rock,
my retreat in every shock,
stronghold, citadel and height,
grace and mercy, life and light,
my deliverer, sacred shore,
teaching me to fight and war,
strengthening my heart and hands,
beating down the warring clans.
Blessed, the people, who are dear,
serving God, the Lord, in fear.

What are we, that you should know,
or consider us below?
Humankind is only mist;
like a shadow we exist.
Lord, descend from heaven above,
strike the mountains and reprove;
as the smoke ascends on high,
lightnings flash and arrows fly.
Blessed, the people, who are dear,
serving God, the Lord, in fear.

Send your hand to set me free,
send your hand, deliver me
from the waters of the flood,
from the hordes of foreign blood,
their deceit and wicked ways,
lying words and empty praise.
I will sing of your repute,
playing well the harp and lute.
Blessed, the people, who are dear,
serving God, the Lord, in fear.

You, who save the lives of kings,
keeping them beneath your wings,
David, free from evil sword,
foreign blood and evil horde;
free me from their wicked ways,
lying words and empty praise,
from the plots of wicked hands,
their deceit and evil plans.
Blessed, the people, who are dear,
serving God, the Lord, in fear.

Sons will grow as tall as pines,
daughters, statuesque and fine,
garners full of harvest yield,
flocks by thousand in our fields,
oxen safely giving birth,
no unrighteousness or dearth,
no lament in town or square,
no injustice anywhere.
Blessed, the people, who are dear,
serving God, the Lord, in fear.

Psalm 145 (An Alphabetic Psalm)
LM
Old Hundredth

All praise to you, my God and King,
I bless your name for evermore,
blessing you daily, as I sing,
praising your name for evermore.

Come, praise the Lord, for he is great,
splendour that we can never gauge.
Daily proclaim his awesome state,
through generations, age to age.

Echo his glory and renown;
I contemplate your wonders, Lord,
for we commend your awesome crown,
and I recount your strength abroad.

Goodness and greatness they record,
singing of all your righteousness.
Holy and gracious is the Lord,
slow in his anger, swift to bless.

In his compassion he is good,
gentle to all beneath his gaze.
Joyful, the faithful firmly stood,
praising the Lord in all his ways.

Kingdom and glory, might and grace -
they will recount your great renown,
laying before the human race,
how splendid are your reign and crown.

More lasting than eternal spheres,
you, Lord, will reign from age to age;
never unfaithful through the years,
holy and true on every stage.

Often as we are bent and poor,
you, Lord, are there to help and raise,
proving your love with food to store;
as we await your loving gaze.

Ready with open hand to fill,
meeting desire, our every need,
surely the Lord is righteous still,
faithful and true in every deed.

To all who call him, he is near,
to all who call with honest goals;
urged by the needs of those who fear,
hearing their cry, he saves their souls.

Vile, wicked folk, he will erase,
keeping the ones who still adore.
While to the Lord I offer praise,
all flesh will bless him evermore.

Psalm 146
77 77 and Alleluias
Llanfair, Easter Hymn

Praise the Lord, my soul and heart, alleluia,
making music, every part, alleluia.
I will sing with every breath, alleluia,
praise my God until my death, alleluia.

Do not trust the high and brave, alleluia,
human powers, who cannot save, alleluia.
When they die, they turn to earth, alleluia,
plans decay in dust and dearth, alleluia.

Blessed are all who hope in God, alleluia,
Jacob's Lord, their help and rod; alleluia,
he made heaven and earth and sea, alleluia,
all their fulness by decree, alleluia.

Keeping truth for evermore, alleluia,
he gives justice to the poor, alleluia,
offering food to those in need; alleluia;
every prisoner shall be freed, alleluia.

He, the Lord, restores our eyes, alleluia,
lifts the bowed who cannot rise, alleluia,
loves the righteous, who are bound, alleluia,
keeping strangers safe and sound, alleluia.

Orphans, widows he restores, alleluia,
but the wicked he deplores, alleluia.
He is King on every stage, alleluia,
Zion's God from age to age, alleluia.

Psalm 147 Part 1
77 77 with Alleluia
Württemberg, Orientis Partibus

Music to the Lord is right,
praising him is our delight,
who rebuilds Jerusalem,
gathering Israel, all of them. Alleluia.

Banished, broken hearts he cures,
binding injuries and sores,
counting every star above,
every name, and how they move. Alleluia.

God, the Lord, is great in might,
lasting truth, eternal light,
saves the humble from their dearth,
casts the wicked down to earth. Alleluia.

Sing to God, the Lord, with praise,
offer thanks in all your days,
melody on harp and lyre,
making music to inspire. Alleluia.

For he fills the heaven with cloud;
earth is covered like a shroud;
his the rain and cooling shower,
making mountain grasses flower. Alleluia.

He gives food to beast and bird,
feeds the ravens by his word,
takes no pleasure in a horse,
powerful legs or human force. Alleluia.

God, the Lord, is good and right;
those who fear are his delight,
those who wait for love and grace,
hope in him and seek his face. Alleluia.

Psalm 147 Part 2
77 77 with Alleluia
Württemberg, Orientis Partibus

Praise the Lord, Jerusalem,
Zion, praise your God again,
who made firm your bars and gates,
blessed your children and estates. Alleluia.

He makes peace in your domain,
filling you with finest grain,
sends his word on earth below,
running swiftly here to grow. Alleluia.

Who can stand his freezing gust,
when he scatters ice as dust,
wooly snow upon the ground,
frost as morsels all around? Alleluia

When he speaks, the breezes blow,
making frozen waters flow.
Jacob carries out his word,
every statute of the Lord. Alleluia.

Other nations on the earth
do not know his laws or worth.
Only Israel fears the Lord,
publishing his works abroad. Alleluia.

Psalm 148
88 34 88 and Alleluias
Laßt uns erfreuen

Praise God, the Lord, you heavens on high,
praise him you heights above the sky.
O praise him, alleluia.
Praise him, you angels who attend,
praise him, his armies who contend.
O praise him, O praise him,
alleluia, alleluia, alleluia.

Praise him, you sun, and moon by night,
praise him, you shining stars of light.
O praise him, alleluia.
Praise him; let highest heaven respond,
and you, the waters far beyond.
O praise him, O praise him,
alleluia, alleluia, alleluia.

May they adore his holy name;
by his decree they will remain.
O praise him, alleluia.
They were created and will stand
for evermore, by his command.
O praise him, O praise him,
alleluia, alleluia, alleluia.

Praise God, the Lord, from earth as well,
sea monster, deep and ocean swell.
O praise him, alleluia.
You fiery smoke, you hail and snow,
and, at his word, you winds that blow,
O praise him, O praise him,
alleluia, alleluia, alleluia.

You mountains and you hills, agree,
cedars and every fruiting tree,
O praise him, alleluia.
All living creatures, wild and tame,
all creeping things and all you game,
O praise him, O praise him,
alleluia, alleluia, alleluia.

Peoples and kings, acclaim his worth,
judges and princes of the earth.
O praise him, alleluia.
Maidens and men with single voice,
elders and children, all rejoice,
O praise him, O praise him,
alleluia, alleluia, alleluia.

May they sing praises to the Lord;
his name alone will be adored.
O praise him, alleluia.
His name and majesty are high
over the earth, above the sky.
O praise him, O praise him,
alleluia, alleluia, alleluia.

He gives his people power and sway,
praise for his faithful folk today -
O praise him, alleluia -
praise for his people, who are near,
children of Israel, who are dear.
O praise him, O praise him,
alleluia, alleluia, alleluia.

Psalm 149

77 77 with Alleluia
Orientis Partibus, Württemberg

Sing a song before the Lord,
new and fresh with every chord,
praise your maker, faithful ones,
Zion's daughters and her sons. Alleluia.

Israel, rejoice and sing,
come, be glad before your king.
Let them praise him and acclaim,
making music to his name. Alleluia.

Praise him, dancing in the choir,
playing timbrel, harp and lyre,
for the Lord delights to know
all his people, high and low. Alleluia.

He adorns the poor who cry,
with his victory from on high.
Let the faithful shout and fear,
celebrate his glory here. Alleluia.

On their beds, he calms their fears,
he, the Father of the Years;
in their mouth he is adored,
in their hand a sharpened sword. Alleluia.

Working victory by their hand,
he rebukes in every land,
binding kings with heavy chains,
crushing every vile campaign. Alleluia.

This, the judgement of the Lord,
this, their work and their reward,
this, their glory, is decreed,
since his faithful ones are freed. Alleluia.

Psalm 150

77 77 and Alleluias
Easter Hymn, Llanfair

Praise the Father of the Years, alleluia!
Praise him in his holy spheres, alleluia!
Praise him in his mighty deeds, alleluia!
Praise him as his power proceeds, alleluia!

Praise him with the blasting horn, alleluia!
May the harp and lyre adorn, alleluia!
Praise him in the rhythmic dance, alleluia!
May the strings and pipe enhance, alleluia!

Praise him with a cymbal clash, alleluia!
Praise him with a cymbal crash, alleluia!
Everything that breathes, adore, alleluia,
praise the Lord for evermore, alleluia!

Alphabetical Index of Tunes

Metrical Index of Tunes

66 84 D
Leoni   18

664 6664
Moscow   93
Olivet   62

665 665 786
Jesu, Meine Freude   12

666 66 and Refrain
Personent Hodie (Theodoric)   7

SM
Franconia   11, 121
Narenza   11
St. Ethelwald   24
St. Paul's (Stainer)   54
Trentham   42, 43

74 74 D
Gwalchmai   101

76 76 D
Au fort de ma détresse   35
King's Lynn   44, 82, 86
Passion Chorale   88
Thornbury   129

76 76 and Refrain
Wir Pflügen   46

77 77
Aus der Tiefe (Heinlein)   64
Monkland   105 without Alleluias
Nottingham   105 without Alleluias
Vienna   75

77 77 and Alleluias
Easter Hymn   146, 150
Llanfair   146, 150

Solomon	119.65-72
Song 67	119.9-16
Southwell (Irons)	119.49-56
St. Botolph	119.145-152
St. Flavian	119.169-176
St. Fulbert	119.89-96
St. James	119.129-136
St. Magnus	119.153-160
St. Nicholas (Greene)	52
St. Peter	119.1-8
St. Stephen	119.161-168
Stockton	119.41-48
Stracathro	119.97-104
Tallis's Ordinal	119.137-144
Westminster	16

DCM

Christmas Carol (Walford Davies)	40, 70, 89 Part 1
Coe Fen	139
First Mode Melody	31, 78, 109
Kingsfold	78
Third Mode Melody	39, 78, 89 Part 2, 130

86 88 6

Logan (suegilmurray@icloud.com)	Nunc Dimittis
Repton	Nunc Dimittis, 56

87 87 33 7

Michael	Benedictus, 72

87 87 77

All Saints	32

87 87 87

Mannheim	22
Neander (Unser Herrscher)	66
Oriel	140
Pange Lingua	90
Picardy	22
Regent Square	103

Finlandia   17, 58
Song 1   63, 77
Unde et Memores   26, 94

10 10 11 11
Laudate Dominum (Parry)   96

10 11 11 12
Slane   95

10 4 10 4 10 10
Alberta   4
Sandon   4

10 4 66 66 10 4
Luckington   8

11 10 11 10
O Perfect Love   45
Strength and Stay   45

11 10 11 10 11 10 11 12
Londonderry Air   41, 138

11 11 11 11
St. Denio   50

11 11 11 5
Cloisters   69
Herzliebster Jesu   51
Iste Confessor   69

13 13 13 13 13 13
Thaxted   Te Deum, 49, 104, 132

14 14 4 7 8
Lobe Den Herren   99

Irregular
St. Patrick   29 vv.1,2,3,5

Index of Uses

Grace and Providence
2, 3, 7, 9, 10, 13, 14, 16, 18, 19, 20, 21, 23, 24, 27, 28, 29, 32, 33, 34, 37, 40, 46, 48, 53, 62, 65, 70, 72, 73, 85, 95, 98, 99, 102, 103, 104, 105, 107, 111, 113, 114, 115, 118, 119, 124, 125, 127, 132, 135, 136, 139, 141, 143, 144, 145, 146, 147, 148, 149, 150

Joy, Praise and Thanksgiving
8, 16, 18, 19, 22, 23, 24, 25, 27, 29, 32, 45, 47, 57, 65, 66, 67, 81, 87, 89, 92, 93, 95, 96, 97, 98, 100, 103, 108, 110, 111, 112, 115, 117, 118, 126, 128, 134, 138, 143, 144, 145, 146, 147, 148, 149, 150

Faith, Trust and Commitment
1, 2, 3, 4, 5, 6, 9, 10, 11, 12, 13, 14, 15, 16, 17, 18, 19, 20, 21, 22, 25, 26, 27, 30, 34, 36, 37, 39, 40, 41, 43, 53, 55, 56, 59, 60, 61, 62, 63, 64, 67, 68, 70, 71, 73, 81, 84, 86, 89, 90, 91, 94, 99, 101, 106, 107, 110, 112, 114, 115, 118, 119, 121, 124, 125, 127, 128, 130, 131, 133, 138, 139, 141, 142, 143

Temptation, Penitence and Forgiveness
18, 19, 22, 25, 30, 31, 32, 38, 49, 50, 51, 78, 81, 88, 95, 96, 97, 103, 107, 109, 121, 141

Hope and Consolation
4, 6, 11, 15, 16, 18, 22, 23, 25, 27, 30, 31, 34, 36, 37, 39, 40, 42, 43, 55, 62, 63, 66, 69, 71, 74, 80, 84, 91, 94, 102, 108, 113, 116, 119, 121, 122, 123, 126, 130, 138, 139, 140, 141, 142, 143

Healing
6, 16, 19, 22, 32, 38, 39, 41, 51, 60, 107, 113, 116, 130, 142

Suffering and Sorrow
6, 12, 13, 14, 22, 26, 31, 35, 38, 39, 41, 42, 43, 44, 51, 53, 55, 59, 60, 61, 64, 69, 71, 74, 77, 78, 79, 80, 86, 88, 89, 102, 109, 116, 120, 123, 130, 137, 140, 143

Protection

5, 7, 9, 10, 12, 16, 20, 21, 22, 25, 27, 28, 31, 35, 46, 48, 54, 56, 59, 62, 68, 70, 71, 76, 80, 83, 86, 91, 93, 108, 134, 139, 140, 142, 144

Redemption and Salvation

1, 6, 8, 14, 15, 18, 22, 25, 30, 35, 38, 50, 51, 53, 54, 60, 66, 68, 78, 103, 105, 106, 114, 116, 118, 124, 126, 129, 130, 135, 136, 141, 143, 144

Pilgrimage

3, 15, 23, 24, 26, 42, 43, 61, 78, 84, 87, 100, 105, 106, 121, 122, 132, 134, 135, 136

Christian Unity

133

Home and Family

24, 45, 55, 90, 101, 104, 113, 122, 125, 127, 128, 131, 133, 144

The Nation

20, 21, 72, 110

Creation

33, 65, 67, 74, 77, 85, 89, 93, 97, 98, 104, 135, 136

Justice

2, 7, 9, 10, 11, 12, 17, 20, 21, 26, 28, 33, 35, 36, 37, 41, 44, 46, 48, 49, 50, 52, 57, 58, 59, 64, 72, 73, 75, 76, 77, 79, 82, 86, 92, 94, 101, 109, 110, 120, 123, 129, 137, 140, 143, 149

Morning

3, 5, 8, 19, 24, 29, 33, 36, 42, 43, 47, 48, 51, 57, 63, 65, 67, 77, 80, 81, 84, 85, 86, 87, 90, 92, 93, 95, 96, 97, 98, 99, 100, 101, 103, 108, 117, 118, 119.145-152, 135, 143, 144, 145, 146, 147, 148, 149, 150

During the Day

7, 13, 14, 17, 19, 22, 23, 25, 26, 28, 34, 40, 45, 53, 54, 55, 56, 57, 59, 60, 61, 64, 70, 71, 74, 75, 76, 79, 80, 82, 88, 94, 118, 119, 120, 121, 122, 123, 124, 125, 126, 127, 128, 129, 130, 131, 133, 140

Evening
11, 15, 16, 20, 21, 27, 30, 32, 41, 45, 46, 49, 62, 67, 72, 110, 111, 112, 113, 114, 115, 116, 119.105-112, 121, 122, 123, 124, 125, 126, 127, 130, 131, 132, 135, 136, 137, 138, 139, 141, 142, 144, 145
Night
4, 16, 31, 86, 88, 91, 130, 134, 139, 143
Advent
9, 11, 12, 14, 25, 28, 40, 44, 50, 62, 68, 72, 75, 76, 80, 85, 89, 113, 122, 123, 126, 131, 144, 146
Christmas
8, 62, 87, 96, 97, 98, 105, 132, 135, 147, 148
New Year and Anniversaries
77, 90
Epiphany
19, 24, 27, 29, 33, 34, 36, 40, 46, 47, 48, 71, 72, 89, 96, 97, 111, 113, 118, 122, 128, 132, 139, 145, 146
Lent
11, 12, 13, 14, 18, 19, 22, 23, 25, 26, 27, 28, 30, 31, 32, 38, 40, 46, 50, 51, 63, 74, 77, 84, 85, 91, 95, 102, 107, 119.1-32, 119.73-88, 119.161-168, 121, 135
Passiontide
22, 25, 27, 30, 31, 34, 35, 36, 39, 41, 42, 43, 51, 55, 61, 62, 69, 70, 71, 80, 86, 88, 102, 107, 111, 112, 116, 118, 119.9-16, 126, 130, 142, 143
Easter
4, 16, 19, 22, 23, 29, 30, 31, 36, 40, 42, 43, 44, 45, 46, 48, 66, 67, 73, 77, 80, 81, 86, 87, 96, 98, 104, 105, 106, 113, 114, 116, 117, 118, 119.89-96, 126, 127, 133, 136, 142, 143, 146, 147, 148, 150
Ascensiontide
1, 8, 15, 24, 47, 68, 76, 93, 97, 99, 104, 110, 147, 150
Pentecost
33, 36, 48, 67, 68, 87, 104, 133, 139, 145, 150
The Holy Trinity
8, 29, 33, 73, 86, 93, 97, 98, 104, 150
Harvest Festival
65, 100, 126

All Saints
1, 5, 15, 24, 32, 33, 34, 43, 84, 87, 111, 112, 117, 119.1-8,
145, 146, 147, 148, 149, 150
Remembrance
17, 20, 40, 46, 62, 70, 82, 90, 91, 136
Patronal Festivals
24, 48, 122, 132, 150
Baptism
29, 36, 46, 47, 89
Confirmation
33, 36, 48, 67, 87, 104, 133, 139, 145, 150
Holy Communion
23, 42, 43, 110, 111, 116, 147
Marriage
45, 127, 128, 133
Funerals
23, 90, 116, 130, 143

Psalms Used in the Common Worship Lectionary

With the exception of Psalm 119 I have only made reference here to whole psalms that occur in any of the three lectionary years or any of the three services for each Sunday. Hence there are several psalms to choose from each Sunday. For a detailed description of the psalm or portion of psalm used in any particular year, please consult the Common Worship Lectionary.

Advent
First Sunday of Advent
9, 25, 44, 80, 122, 144
Second Sunday of Advent
11, 28, 40, 72, 75, 76, 80, 85
Third Sunday of Advent
12, 14, 50, 62, 68, 126, 146
Fourth Sunday of Advent
80, 89, 113, 123, 126, 131, 144
Christmas Eve
85, 89

Christmas
Christmas Day
8, 62, 96, 97, 98
First Sunday of Christmas
105, 132, 148
Second Sunday of Christmas
87, 135, 147

Epiphany
The Epiphany
72, 96, 97, 113, 132
The Baptism of Christ
29, 36, 46, 47, 89
Second Sunday of Epiphany
36, 40, 96, 139, 145

Third Sunday of Epiphany
19, 27, 33, 113, 128
Fourth Sunday of Epiphany
34, 36, 48, 71, 111
The Presentation of Christ in the Temple
24, 48, 118, 122, 132, 146

Ordinary Time
Proper 1
1, 2, 3, 4, 5, 6, 112, 138, 147
Proper 2
1, 5, 6, 7, 10, 13, 30, 119.1-8
Proper 3
10, 11, 13, 18, 21, 23, 33, 37, 41, 119.33-40
Second Sunday before Lent
29, 65, 67, 100, 104, 136, 147, 148, 150
Sunday next before Lent
2, 27, 50, 72, 84, 89, 99, 150

Lent
Ash Wednesday
38, 51, 102
First Sunday of Lent
25, 32, 50, 77, 91, 119.1-32, 119.73-88
Second Sunday of Lent
22, 27, 51, 74, 119.161-168, 121, 135
Third Sunday of Lent
11, 12, 13, 18, 19, 26, 28, 40, 46, 63, 95
Fourth Sunday of Lent
13, 14, 19, 23, 27, 30, 31, 32, 84, 85, 107
Mothering Sunday
34, 127
Fifth Sunday of Lent
30, 34, 35, 51, 86, 107, 111, 112, 119.9-16, 126, 130
Palm Sunday
31, 61, 62, 69, 80, 118

Monday of Holy Week
25, 36, 41
Tuesday of Holy Week
27, 55, 71
Wednesday of Holy Week
70, 88, 102
Maundy Thursday
39, 42, 43, 116
Good Friday
22, 69, 130, 143
Easter Eve
116, 142

Easter
Easter Vigil
16, 19, 42, 43, 46, 98, 114, 136, 143
Easter Day
66, 105, 114, 117, 118
Second Sunday of Easter
16, 22, 30, 81, 118, 133, 136, 143, 150
Third Sunday of Easter
4, 23, 30, 48, 77, 80, 86, 116, 142
Fourth Sunday of Easter
23, 29, 81, 106, 113, 114, 119.89-96, 146
Fifth Sunday of Easter
16, 22, 30, 31, 44, 96, 98, 147, 148
Sixth Sunday of Easter
36, 40, 45, 66, 67, 73, 87, 98, 104, 126, 127
Ascension Day
8, 15, 24, 47, 93, 110, 150
Seventh Sunday of Easter
1, 47, 68, 76, 97, 99, 104, 147
Pentecost
33, 36, 48, 67, 87, 104, 133, 139, 145, 150

Psalms for the Common Era

Ordinary Time
Trinity Sunday
8, 29, 33, 73, 86, 93, 97, 98, 104, 150
Day of Thanksgiving for Holy Communion
23, 42, 43, 110, 111, 116, 147
Proper 4
28, 31, 32, 33, 35, 37, 39, 41, 46, 81, 96, 139
Proper 5
30, 33, 36, 37, 38, 39, 41, 44, 45, 50, 130, 138, 146
Proper 6
5, 20, 32, 39, 42, 43, 45, 49, 52, 53, 92, 100, 116
Proper 7
9, 22, 42, 43, 46, 48, 49, 50, 55, 57, 69, 86, 107, 133
Proper 8
13, 16, 30, 50, 52, 53, 56, 59, 60, 64, 77, 89, 130
Proper 9
30, 45, 48, 55, 56, 57, 63, 64, 65, 66, 70, 74, 123, 145
Proper 10
24, 25, 60, 63, 64, 65, 66, 76, 77, 82, 85, 119.105-112
Proper 11
15, 23, 52, 67, 70, 71, 73, 81, 82, 86, 89, 100, 139
Proper 12
14, 74, 75, 76, 77, 85, 88, 95, 105, 119.129-136, 128, 138, 145
Proper 13
17, 49, 51, 78, 80, 85, 86, 88, 106, 107, 145
Proper 14
33, 34, 50, 85, 86, 88, 90, 91, 105, 108, 115, 116, 130
Proper 15
34, 67, 80, 82, 90, 92, 100, 106, 111, 119.17-48, 133
Proper 16
34, 71, 84, 95, 103, 104, 115, 116, 119.49-88, 124, 138
Proper 17
15, 26, 45, 81, 105, 107, 112, 119.1-40, 119.81-96, 119.161-176
Proper 18
1, 108, 115, 119.17-72, 120, 121, 122, 123, 125, 139, 146, 149

Proper 19
14, 19, 51, 103, 114, 116, 119.41-88, 119.105-120, 124, 125, 126, 127
Proper 20
1, 54, 79, 105, 113, 119.1-8, 119.113-176, 128, 129, 130, 131, 145
Proper 21
19, 25, 78, 91, 120, 121, 122, 123, 124, 125, 126, 127, 132, 134, 135, 146
Proper 22
8, 19, 26, 37, 80, 123, 124, 125, 126, 128, 129, 134, 136, 141, 142, 137
Proper 23
22, 23, 66, 90, 106, 111, 127, 128, 129, 130, 138, 139, 141, 143, 144
Proper 24
91, 96, 99, 104, 119.97-104, 121, 133, 134, 137, 141, 142, 143, 145, 146, 147, 149
Proper 25
1, 34, 65, 84, 90, 119.1-16, 119.89-152, 126
Bible Sunday
19, 119.1-16, 119.89-152
All Saints' Day
1, 5, 15, 24, 34, 84, 148, 149, 150
Fourth Sunday before Advent
32, 33, 43, 87, 111, 112, 117, 119.1-8, 145, 149
Third Sunday before Advent
17, 20, 40, 46, 62, 70, 82, 90, 91, 136
Second Sunday before Advent
16, 89, 90, 93, 95, 96, 97, 98, 132
Christ the King
29, 46, 72, 93, 95, 97, 99, 100, 110

Festivals
The Naming and Circumcision of Jesus (1 January)
8, 103, 115, 148, 150

The Conversion of St. Paul (25 January)
66, 67, 119.41-56, 147, 149
Joseph of Nazareth (19 March)
1, 25, 89, 112, 132, 147
The Annunciation of Our Lord (25 March)
40, 85, 111, 113, 131, 146
George (23 April)
3, 5, 11, 111, 116, 126, 146
Mark (25 April)
19, 37, 45, 119.9-16, 148
Philip and James (1 May)
25, 119.1-8, 139, 146, 149
Matthias (14 May)
15, 16, 80, 147
The Visit of the Blessed Virgin Mary to Elizabeth (31 May)
45, 85, 113, 122, 127, 128, 150
Barnabas (11 June)
1, 15, 100, 101, 112, 117, 147
The Birth of John the Baptist (24 June)
50, 71, 80, 82, 85, 149
Peter and Paul (29 June)
66, 67, 71, 113, 124, 125, 138
Thomas (3 July)
27, 31, 92, 139, 146
Mary Magdalen (22 July)
30, 32, 42, 63, 139, 150
James (25 July)
7, 29, 94, 117, 126, 144
The Transfiguration of Our Lord (6 August)
27, 72, 97, 99, 110, 150
The Blessed Virgin Mary (15 August)
45, 72, 98, 132, 138, 147
Bartholomew (24 August)
86, 91, 97, 116, 117, 145
Holy Cross Day (14 September)
2, 8, 22, 66, 110, 146, 150

Matthew (21 September)
34, 49, 117, 119.33-40, 119.65-72, 119.89-96
Michael and All Angels (29 September)
34, 91, 103, 138, 148, 150
Luke (18 October)
33, 103, 145, 146, 147
Simon and Jude (28 October)
116, 117, 119.1-16, 119.89-96, 124, 125, 126
Andrew (30 November)
19, 47, 48, 87, 96, 147
Stephen (26 December)
13, 31, 57, 86, 119.161-168, 150
John (27 December)
21, 97, 117, 147
The Holy Innocents (28 December)
36, 123, 124, 128, 146
Dedication Festival
24, 48, 122, 132, 150
Harvest Thanksgiving
65, 100, 126

Printed in Great Britain
by Amazon